Guidelines for Marine Protected Areas

IUCN – The World Conservation Union

Founded in 1948, The World Conservation Union brings together States, government agencies and a diverse range of non-governmental organizations in a unique world partnership: over 900 members in all, spread across some 138 countries.

As a Union, IUCN seeks to influence, encourage and assist societies throughout the world to conserve the integrity and diversity of nature and to ensure that any use of natural resources is equitable and ecologically sustainable. A central secretariat coordinates the IUCN Programme and serves the Union membership, representing their views on the world stage and providing them with the strategies, services, scientific knowledge and technical support they need to achieve their goals. Through its six Commissions, IUCN draws together over 10,000 expert volunteers in project teams and action groups, focusing in particular on species and biodiversity conservation and the management of habitats and natural resources. The Union has helped many countries to prepare National Conservation Strategies, and demonstrates the application of its knowledge through the field projects it supervises. Operations are increasingly decentralized and are carried forward by an expanding network of regional and country offices, located principally in developing countries.

The World Conservation Union builds on the strengths of its members, networks and partners to enhance their capacity and to support global alliances to safeguard natural resources at local, regional and global levels.

Cardiff University

The Department of City and Regional Planning, Cardiff University is pleased to be a partner in the production of this important series of guidelines for protected area planning and management. The Department, through its Environmental Planning Research Unit, is actively involved in protected areas research; runs specialised courses on planning and environmental policy; and has a large Graduate School offering opportunities for persons interested in pursuing research for a PhD or as part of wider career development. If you are interested in learning more about the Department, its research capabilities and courses please write to us at the address given below.

Professor Terry Marsden BAHon., PhD, MRTPI
Head of Department
Department of City and Regional Planning
Cardiff University
Glamorgan Building
King Edward VIIth Avenue
Cardiff, CFl0 3WA, Wales, UK

Tel: + 44 02920 874022
Fax: + 44 02920 874845
Email: MarsdenTK@cf.ac.uk
Web site: www.cf.ac.uk

Guidelines for Marine Protected Areas

World Commission on Protected Areas of
IUCN – The World Conservation Union

Edited and coordinated by Graeme Kelleher

Series Editor: Adrian Phillips

With the support of:
Coastal Zone Management Centre, The Hague, The Netherlands
The Department of City and Regional Planning, Cardiff University,
Wales, UK
The National Oceanic and Atmospheric Administration,
US Department of Commerce
Countryside Council for Wales, UK

World Commission on Protected Areas

Best Practice Protected Area Guidelines Series No. 3

IUCN – The World Conservation Union
1999

The designation of geographical entities in this book, and the presentation of the material, do not imply the expression of any opinion whatsoever on the part of IUCN, Cardiff University, Countryside Council for Wales, National Oceanic and Atmospheric Administration or the Coastal Zone Management Centre concerning the legal status of any country, territory, or area, or of its authorities, or concerning the delimitation of its frontiers or boundaries. Furthermore, the views expressed in this publication do not necessarily reflect those of IUCN, CCW, NOAA, the CZM Centre or Cardiff University.

This publication has been made possible in large part by funding from Cardiff University, CCW, NOAA, the CZM Centre and IUCN.

Published by:	IUCN, Gland, Switzerland, and Cambridge, UK.
Copyright:	© 1999 International Union for the Conservation of Nature and Natural Resources
	Reproduction of this publication for educational or other non-commercial purposes is authorized without prior written permission from the copyright holder provided the source is fully acknowledged.
	Reproduction of this publication for resale or other commercial purposes is prohibited without prior written permission of the copyright holders.
Citation:	Kelleher, G. (1999). *Guidelines for Marine Protected Areas*. IUCN, Gland, Switzerland and Cambridge, UK. xxiv +107pp.
ISBN:	2-8317-0505-3
Cover design by:	IUCN Publications Services Unit
Cover photos:	Front cover, NOAA; back cover, Jan Post
Layout by:	IUCN Publications Services Unit
Produced by:	IUCN Publications Services Unit, Cambridge, UK
Printed by:	Black Bear Press Ltd, Cambridge, UK
Available from:	IUCN Publications Services Unit 219c Huntingdon Road, Cambridge CB3 0DL, United Kingdom Tel: ++44 1223 277894 Fax: ++44 1223 277175 E-mail: info@books.iucn.org www: http://www.iucn.org A catalogue of IUCN publications is also available

The text of this book is printed on 90gsm Fineblade Cartridge made from low-chlorine pulp.

Table of Contents

Foreword

The aim of these Guidelines is to help countries establish systems of Marine Protected Areas (MPAs), as a key component of integrated management of their coastal and marine areas and as part of their sustainable development.

Creation and effective management of MPAs have lagged behind those of protected areas on land, but are just as important. MPAs are a vital part of broader programmes to conserve the marine heritage and life-support system of the world, and to ensure that where living marine resources are used, that use can be sustained ecologically. The world urgently needs a comprehensive system of MPAs to conserve biodiversity and to help rebuild the productivity of the oceans. MPAs can help achieve the three main objectives of living resource conservation as defined in the World Conservation Strategy (IUCN, 1980):

- to maintain essential ecological processes and life support systems;

- to preserve genetic diversity; and

- to ensure the sustainable utilization of species and ecosystems.

These guidelines set out the various actions needed to make an effective MPA, from the early planning stages to implementation. However, they do not deal in detail with every operational aspect of the day-to-day management of MPAs. Nor, for reasons of length, do they provide guidance on integrated coastal management, even though that is the broader context within which MPAs should be managed.

We want these guidelines to be useful to natural resource managers at all levels, whether working on conservation of nature or sustainable use of marine resources. They therefore contain material of help to policy-makers, planners and field managers.

These guidelines replace those published by IUCN in 1991. They are part of a set of recent documents on MPAs prepared by IUCN's World Commission on Protected Areas (WCPA). The others are:

- *A Global Representative System of Marine Protected Areas*. Principal editors Graeme Kelleher, Chris Bleakley and Sue Wells. Great Barrier Reef Marine Park Authority, The World Bank and IUCN. 4 vols (1995). Analysis of existing MPA coverage and proposals on where MPAs are needed for each region of the world, with priority actions identified regionally and globally.

- An issue of *PARKS* magazine (Volume 8, No. 2, 1998) devoted to management of MPAs, with emphasis on the links to fisheries management and the application of protected area categories to MPAs.

Much has happened since the first edition of the guidelines came out in 1991. The concept of MPAs is much more widely appreciated and the need for a global network of MPAs is now generally accepted. There is a flurry of MPA initiatives around the world. The United Nations Convention on the Law of the Sea (UNCLOS) and the Convention on Biological Diversity (CBD) oblige countries to protect the marine environment. Yet large effective MPAs are still very rare and the network remains woefully small by comparison with what is needed. May these guidelines help to accelerate action and lead to greater success in MPA establishment and management around the world.

We call on governments around the world to take to heart the various international conventions and IUCN resolutions they have adopted on MPAs and convert these into concrete action. We urge local communities and NGOs to assist in this process. We invite international bodies, in particular UNESCO, UNEP, UNDP, the World Bank and the Global Environmental Facility, as well as WWF and IUCN, to increase their essential support and encouragement to this process. The IUCN-WCPA network of MPA experts stands ready to give all the help it can in this important task.

Graeme Kelleher
Nancy Foster

Acknowledgements

We are grateful to all those who have contributed text to these guidelines, particularly Grazia Borrini-Feyerabend and Meriwether Wilson, as well as those who contributed to the earlier version. We also thanks those who have made constructive criticisms and suggestions, particularly Sofia Bettencourt, Leah Bunce, Françoise Burhenne, Adam Cole-King, Charles "Bud" Ehler, Keith Foster, Scott Frazier, Brian Groombridge, Jeremy Harrison, Lee Kimball, Barbara Lausche, J. Mathias, Francine Mercier, Olav Nord-Varhaug, Bernadette O'Neil, Jeanne Pagnan, Cassandra Phillips, Dianeetha Sadacharan, David Sheppard, Clare Shine, M.S. Swaminathan, Kathy Walls, Sue Wells and Meriwether Wilson. All their comments, suggestions and criticisms have been taken into account, but the opinions expressed are of course our own, except where we quote from others, and errors and omissions are our responsibility. We thank Hugh Synge for help with editing.

Graeme Kelleher and Nancy Foster

Executive Summary

Marine Protected Areas (MPAs) are essential to conserve the biodiversity of the oceans and to maintain productivity, especially of fish stocks. Yet at present there are too few MPAs and not many of them are effectively managed. These guidelines set out the various steps a country should take to establish an effective network of MPAs.

IUCN has defined an MPA as "any area of intertidal or subtidal terrain, together with its overlying water and associated flora, fauna, historical and cultural features, which has been reserved by law or other effective means to protect part or all of the enclosed environment".

There are two ways of establishing MPA systems: either as many relatively small sites, each strictly protected, or as a few large multiple-use areas which contain strictly protected areas within them. To conserve biodiversity, both approaches should occur within an effective programme of ecosystem management covering the marine ecosystem and the land areas that affect it.

From the accumulated technical experience in this field, there is one general lesson which can be drawn. A crucial attribute of an MPA manager is integrity. Some managers have made the mistake of believing that they can fool some of the people some, or even all, of the time. The result is a breakdown in trust. The manager may appear to win a series of battles but in fact the eventual outcome is failure.

Another key lesson is that time spent in preparation is an essential investment that will be repaid many times over. Proponents of MPAs have to show demonstrable benefits for stakeholders, and this takes time and diplomacy. Box 1 lists other lessons from experience in establishing and managing MPAs in various situations around the world.

The Guidelines set out the following steps, each being the subject of a separate chapter:

1. **Placing MPAs in their wider context**. The high degree of linkage between land and adjoining sea, and the inter-connectivity of the oceans, require that MPAs be integrated into management regimes that deal with all human activities that affect marine life. Thus MPAs should be integrated with other policies for land use and use of the sea. It is also desirable for countries to make use of international agreements, notably UNCLOS and CBD. More international support is needed for MPAs and more attempts should be made to establish MPAs on the High Seas.

2. **Developing the legal framework**. In most countries, a key step will be to establish the legislation needed. This may either be enabling legislation, which allows the administration or communities to establish individual MPAs, or specific legislation establishing an MPA, usually as a large multiple-use area. The various requirements for the legislation are outlined, though the needs and context will differ from one country to another.

3. **Working with relevant sectors**. Many sectors of human activity affect the coast and the sea, and it is vital for those planning an MPA to work with these sectors from the earliest opportunity. Tourism often has most to gain from an MPA and can generate the greatest economic activity from it. Fisheries is the other key sector, and one with which it is most important to cooperate. Other relevant sectors include aquaculture, coastal development, agriculture, forestry, industry, defence and science.

4. **Making partnerships with communities and other stakeholders**. MPA management should understand the local communities that will be affected by the MPA and identify potential partners. It must listen to the many interests and seek ways to involve them as participants in resource management. It is recommended to build management partnerships using the collaborative management model, which is outlined in greater detail in Annex 1.

5. **Selecting the sites for MPAs**. Choosing the location and extent of MPAs involves a different emphasis to that of terrestrial protected areas. In many parts of the world, local people depend greatly on the services and resources provided by natural terrestrial areas. However, the dependence on marine areas tends to be even greater. Some forms of fishing can occur in large areas without threatening the conservation objectives of the MPA because they do not involve habitat modification. This makes it feasible to balance conservation and the needs of local people. Weight needs to be given to events outside the MPA that might affect it, such as pollution. Following these principles, the guidelines propose a rigorous set of criteria for site selection that have been applied in many countries over the past few years.

6. **Planning and managing the MPA**. Management should be responsive and adaptive, working with local interests in a way that builds support for the conservation objectives. To achieve this, managers should adopt a systems approach, use interdisciplinary teams and follow a clear sequence of decision-making. Most MPA management is about managing human activities, so this must be at the heart of the approach. Suggested contents for a management plan are provided in Annex 2.

7. **Zoning**, in which various areas are allocated for various uses. This is usually the best way of ensuring strict protection of a core zone as part of a larger, multiple-use area. The stages involved in preparing a zoning plan are outlined in Annex 3.

8. **Planning for financial sustainability**. Lack of funds is a critical problem for many MPAs. Managers therefore need the freedom to raise funds in as many ways as possible, such as user fees, donations and environment funds, and to retain those funds for management of the MPA. External donors are advised to extend the aid period for protected area projects, so as to help achieve financial sustainability.

9. **Ensuring research, monitoring, evaluation and review**. Research and monitoring should be firmly orientated to solving management issues. Guidance is given on the planning and development of a monitoring and research programme, with its different emphases in the planning and the implementation phase of the MPA. Most important of all is to use the results of research and monitoring to evaluate and if necessary reorient management.

Box 1. Marine Protected Areas – Key Lessons Learnt

■ Almost all MPAs contribute to the maintenance or restitution of both biological diversity and abundance, both of which are relevant to sustainable fisheries;

■ It is not feasible in today's marine environment to divorce the questions of resource use and conservation, because marine natural resources and their living space are all sought now by many different users for many different purposes;

■ The tendency in some areas to oppose the recognition of fishery reserves as MPAs seems to be counterproductive, inhibiting cooperation between fishers and environmentalists in creating and managing MPAs;

■ There has been a long history in almost all areas of the world of conflict and lack of cooperation between environmental and fisheries management agencies. This lack of joint action inhibits progress in establishing MPAs and managing them wherever it is manifest. Individual MPAs and system plans should be designed to serve both sustainable use and environmental protection objectives, and relevant agencies should work together in planning and management;

■ Local people must be deeply involved from the earliest possible stage in any MPA that is to succeed. This involvement should extend to them receiving clearly identifiable benefits from the MPA;

■ Socio-economic considerations usually determine the success or failure of MPAs. In addition to biophysical factors, these considerations should be addressed from the outset in identifying sites for MPAs, and in selecting and managing them;

■ It is better to have an MPA which is not ideal in the ecological sense but which meets the primary objective than to strive vainly to create the 'perfect MPA';

■ It is usually a mistake to postpone action on the establishment of an MPA because biophysical information is incomplete. There will usually be sufficient information to indicate whether the MPA is justified ecologically and to set reasonable boundaries;

■ Design and management of MPAs must be both top-down and bottom-up;

■ An MPA must have clearly defined objectives against which its performance is regularly checked, and a monitoring programme to assess management effectiveness. Management should be adaptive, meaning that it is periodically reviewed and revised as dictated by the results of monitoring;

■ There is a global debate about the merits of small, highly protected MPAs and large, multiple use MPAs. Much of this debate arises from the misconception that it must be one or the other. In fact, nearly all large, multiple use MPAs encapsulate highly protected zones, which can function in the same way as individual highly protected MPAs. Conversely, a small, highly protected MPA in a larger area subject to integrated management can be as effective as a large, multiple use MPA;

■ Because of the highly connected nature of the sea, which efficiently transmits substances and forcing factors, an MPA will rarely succeed unless it is embedded in, or is so large that it constitutes, an integrated ecosystem management regime.

Source: *PARKS* 8(2), 1998

Introduction

We depend on the seas. They feed us and are essential in climate cycles and other global processes that sustain life. They were the source of life on earth and are now home to a vast array of organisms, from a wider range of taxonomic groups than on land. They support a growing tourism and recreation industry. Transport by sea is still the mainstay of world trade. The seas provide a range of novel chemicals for use in medicine. They are an intrinsic part of the culture not just of tribal and coastal people but of all of us. For coastal countries, they are essential to development. In short, the seas are a vital part of the natural and cultural heritage of the world.

Yet throughout the world the seas are suffering degradation. Too many fish are caught, too much rubbish is dumped in the sea, too many pollutants from the land end up there. Bottom-trawling can change habitats over vast areas of the sea-bed: on average, under this practice over 80% of the catch is discarded, most of it dead. In many regions, unsustainable fishing practices are still common, for example using poisons or dynamite.

Threats are most acute in the coastal zone, particularly from increasing human populations. In much of the tropics, marine productivity of the sea is concentrated in small areas of coral reefs, sea-grass beds and mangroves around the coasts, which provide rich feeding and breeding grounds for fish. Coral reefs are particularly at risk, from global warming, mining for building materials, land-based pollution and siltation, over-fishing or destructive fishing and unregulated tourism. While such areas are small in comparison with the open oceans, they are the most diverse and threatened, as well as the source of much of the livelihood of coastal communities.

However, it is a misconception that the only productive parts of the sea are near the coast. Soft-bottom sea areas without hard structures often contain an abundance of sponges, invertebrates, worms, nematodes and algae. These areas badly need protection too.

Conservation efforts for the high seas are caught in the tragedy of open access. The seas are used by everyone but owned by no-one. Usually no single agency or organization in society is responsible for the careful management and conservation of the seas. This makes marine conservation doubly difficult.

If problems exist now, they are likely to be even greater in future because of climate change. The predicted sea-level rise could be devastating to many islands. Pacific and Indian Ocean countries are particularly vulnerable, because of their hundreds of low-lying islands and atolls. The effects will be worst during cyclones, storm surges, king tides and the El Niño fluctuations. The coastline will be more prone to erosion, putting coastal infrastructure at risk. Mangroves will disappear and farmland will be inundated with salt water. A UNEP study has estimated that sea-level rise could cause the Marshall Islands, Kiribati, Tuvalu and Tokelau to cease to exist as nations. In both 1990 and 1991, the largest tides of the year almost inundated the urban area of Majuro in the Marshall Islands. Here is an environmental threat that is putting the survival of whole nations at risk.

One of the marine ecosystems that is most vulnerable to climate change is the coral reef. The rate of sea-level rise can exceed the rate of vertical growth of coral formations. Temperature increases can cause coral bleaching followed by death. However, the vast algal flats, which lie at sea level on the surface of mature coral reefs, may be replaced by living coral as sea level rises, and coral reefs may extend further from the equator as sea temperatures rise.

The impact of climate change is multi-factorial, i.e. biodiversity may be lost as a result of the interaction of different effects. For example, there is some evidence that, if stressed by nutrient levels and/or increased sediments, coral reefs are more vulnerable to temperature changes and increases in ultraviolet radiation. Also, if vegetative cover on land is lost on a large scale, the increased erosion will be very damaging to coral reefs. Increased storm activity, too, will lead to more freshwater run-off, probably including higher erosion and nutrient run-off rates: the resulting lower salinity will adversely affect the coral.

Impacts of climate change are not confined to the tropics. There is already evidence of increased ice-melting rates, salinity changes, shifts in thermoclines and productivity changes. Sea-level rise in many parts of the world will lead to the loss of intertidal habitats such as mangroves, salt marshes and productive mudflats. Changing sea temperatures can lead to changes in the spatial range of marine species. Warm water species can spread polewards, interacting with local species, possibly depleting their numbers or displacing them. The species composition and structure of many marine habitats, particularly in temperate regions, may change.

The big danger is that the rate of climate change and consequent effects on the sea may exceed the adaptive capacity of marine ecosystems.

Why do we need MPAs to conserve the oceans?

Clearly, conservation of the seas is vital, but why MPAs? This question is often asked, especially in the light of what marine scientists term the inter-connectivity of the sea. Fish, algae, nutrients, pollutants and much else besides move freely in the water column. There are few natural boundaries in the oceans. Setting up an MPA will not stop fish moving out nor prevent pollutants moving in.

There are two principal reasons for MPAs: to protect habitat and biodiversity, and to help maintain viable fisheries. (Others are listed in Box 2, which provides a summary of all the benefits of MPAs).

By protecting habitats, MPAs safeguard the vital life-support processes of the sea, including photosynthesis, maintenance of food chains, movement of nutrients, degradation of pollutants and conservation of biological diversity and productivity. They protect both biodiversity and water quality. The protection of marine habitats in their natural state provides an essential foundation for sustainable, nature-based tourism, which is becoming a world industry and provides major benefits to local communities.

MPAs act as an insurance policy for fisheries. The conventional method of conserving fish stocks is to attempt (often unsuccessfully) to control "fishing effort" and total catch, the allowable levels of which are determined from a prediction of fish stocks. But many stocks are unstable and behave in ways that mathematicians term chaotic. For example, a small increase in fishing effort could lead to the collapse of a fishery. It also means that predicting fish stock levels over anything other than short periods will be unreliable. Thus controlling fishing effort and total catch has failed to prevent many fisheries around the world from degradation and even collapse.

MPAs, if partially or entirely closed to fishing, have proved very effective in association with conventional fisheries management in rebuilding damaged fish stocks and in giving all stocks some stability. In several regions, fish stocks have increased rapidly following establishment of MPAs. Far from hurting the fishing industry, the MPAs led to enhanced catches, so providing a direct economic benefit. The larger stocks inside the reserves export their offspring to fishing grounds by ocean currents. Juveniles and adults may also emigrate from the reserves, so boosting nearby fisheries. *PARKS* 8(2) documents several examples.

Box 2. A Summary of the benefits of MPAs

- Conservation of biodiversity, especially critical habitats of threatened species;
- Protection of attractive habitats and species on which sustainable tourism can be based;
- Increased productivity of fisheries by: insurance against stock collapse; buffer against recruitment failure; increase in densities and average sizes of individuals; increase in reproductive output; provide centres for dispersal of propagules and adults (spillover); contain more natural species composition, age structure, spawning potential and genetic variability;
- Contribute to increased knowledge of marine science through information on functional linkages, implementation of the precautionary principle, provision of control sites for research and ecological benchmarks against which to measure human-induced change; potential as nodes in monitoring networks; more "natural" systems where natural mortality can be compared with fishing mortality;
- A refuge for intensely exploited species;
- Protection of genetic diversity of heavily exploited populations;
- Protection of cultural diversity, e.g. sacred places, wrecks and lighthouses.

Adapted from a list developed by Kathy Walls, Dept of Conservation, New Zealand.

Protected areas and MPAs

IUCN defines a protected area as:

> "An area of land and/or sea especially dedicated to the protection of biological diversity, and of natural and associated cultural resources, and managed through legal or other effective means". (IUCN, 1994)

Protected areas are divided into six types, depending on their objectives:

Category I – **Protected area managed mainly for science or wilderness protection** (Strict Nature Reserve/Wilderness Area);

Category II – **Protected area managed mainly for ecosystem protection and recreation** (National Park);

Category III – **Protected area managed mainly for conservation of specific natural features** (Natural Monument);

Category IV – **Protected area managed mainly for conservation through management intervention** (Habitat/Species Management Area);

Category V – **Protected area managed mainly for landscape/seascape conservation and recreation** (Protected Landscape/Seascape);

Category VI – **Protected area managed mainly for the sustainable use of natural ecosystems** (Managed Resource Protected Area). (IUCN, 1994)

PARKS 8(2) gives a range of examples of how MPAs can be categorized under this global system. In addition all but the smallest MPAs are identified in the appropriate category in the *UN List of Protected Areas* (IUCN, 1998).

IUCN has developed a compatible definition of an MPA:

"Any area of intertidal or subtidal terrain, together with its overlying water and associated flora, fauna, historical and cultural features, which has been reserved by law or other effective means to protect part or all of the enclosed environment".

(Resolution 17.38 of the IUCN General Assembly, 1988, reaffirmed in Resolution 19.46 (1994). Both are given in full in Annex 4.)

This language essentially means that:

■ An MPA always includes the marine environment but may also include coastal land areas and islands. It is commonly called an MPA when the total area of sea it encompasses exceeds the area of land within its boundaries, or the marine part of a large protected area is sufficient in size to be classified as an MPA in its own right;

■ It has some form of protection, usually legal but not necessarily. For example, in the Pacific, many MPAs are established by customary tradition;

■ The degree of protection is not necessarily the same throughout the area; indeed most large MPAs are of necessity zoned into areas of different impact and usage;

■ The MPA (and so the provisions for its management) should cover not only the seabed but also at least some of the water column above with its flora and fauna;

■ MPAs are not just relevant for natural features but also for protecting cultural features such as wrecks, historic lighthouses and jetties.

One thing the definition does not say. It does not state that an MPA should keep people out. Indeed, marine conservationists are very keen to challenge the frequent perception that the major aim of MPAs is to exclude people. As these guidelines emphasize, MPAs only work if all the users of the marine environment have a stake in their success. And this usually means some form of managed access for each set of stakeholders.

In practice there is a wide range of types of MPAs. They include MPAs which are:

- Set up under customary tenure (e.g. in the Pacific region);

- Managed on a voluntary basis (e.g. in the UK);

- Developed and operated by the private sector (e.g. Chumbe, Zanzibar, Tanzania);

- Based and run by a local community (e.g. Philippine fishing villages);

- Set up and operated under collaborative management systems (e.g Inuit communities in Canada); and

- Run by government agencies.

In addition, a number of MPAs have international designations, e.g. biosphere reserve, Ramsar site or World Heritage site.

The Goal of MPAs

The goal of MPAs, as seen by IUCN, is to conserve the biological diversity and productivity (including ecological life support systems) of the oceans. Both aspects of the goal are equally important for restoring and maintaining ecosystem health. For instance, conserving an area of relatively low diversity but high productivity, such as a sea grass bed, may be essential to maintaining viable populations of threatened species, such as dugong. In terms of contributing to human welfare, maintaining biological productivity is essential. Correspondingly, most MPAs depend on the support of local communities for survival and such support may well depend on recognition of the contribution which the MPA makes to human welfare through maintaining biological productivity.

While marine conservation and sustainable use are sometimes seen as fundamentally different objectives, they are in fact intimately interrelated. Some MPAs have failed because the only aim of the external sponsor has been biodiversity conservation while that of the local community has been some level of resource use. Both aims can be, and usually are to some extent, reconciled within one MPA, but there needs to be clarity from the outset about how the two sets of objectives relate to each other.

The optimal approach may differ depending on the primary objective. If the primary aim is conservation of a particular species or ecosystem, a large no-take zone may be the best option but if the main aim is sustainable management, work in the Caribbean has shown that a network of smaller sanctuaries may maximize recruitment of fish into surrounding areas.

Experience has shown that there are two broad approaches to creating an MPA system that protects the biodiversity of a complete ecosystem:

- *Either* by establishing a series of relatively small marine protected areas as part of a broader framework of integrated ecosystem management;

- *Or* by establishing a large, multiple zone marine protected area encompassing a complete marine ecosystem or a large part of one.

While either approach is viable, there can be advantages in the latter, because primary responsibility for management of the whole area is likely to be vested in a single agency. In these circumstances integrated management is easier to achieve than when primary responsibility is shared between different agencies, often with different, conflicting priorities.

IUCN has defined the goal for a global network of MPAs in the formal language of its General Assembly Resolutions:

> "To provide for the protection, restoration, wise use, understanding and enjoyment of the marine heritage of the world in perpetuity through the creation of a global, representative system of marine protected areas and through the management in accordance with the principles of the World Conservation Strategy of human activities that use or affect the marine environment".

> (This goal is derived from General Assembly Resolution 17.38 (1988). The same goal is reiterated in General Assembly Resolution 19.46 (1994) and in a similar resolution of the 4th World Wilderness Congress in 1987.)

Some interpretation of this complex text may be helpful:

- **Protection**: The hallmark of an MPA is protection, whether of natural or cultural diversity. Items of biodiversity to be protected might include ecosystems and the species they contain, critical habitats for endangered or economically important species, genetic diversity and particular species. It is most important to prevent outside activities from harming the MPA.

- **Restoration**: To restore threatened species and degraded ecosystems, especially for fisheries.

- **Wise use**: As used in the definition, this term means for the use of people on an ecologically sustainable basis. This includes providing for the continued welfare of people affected by the creation of the MPA. It also usually involves accommodating a broad spectrum of human activities compatible with the primary goal of conservation.

- **Understanding** – otherwise we shall not know how to manage it. Monitoring and research will be required to see if the protection is working.

- **Enjoyment**: If the public are not able to enjoy the MPA, they will not support it. Interpretation facilities may be needed to explain the significance and interest of the MPA.

- **Marine heritage**. This includes:
    - Biodiversity, including the abundance and diversity of marine organisms;
    - Productivity, principally the ability of the system to produce organisms that can be harvested;
    - Cultural and historical elements.

- **In perpetuity**: The aim is to ensure that the protection lasts and is not undermined by insidious and cumulative degradation.

■ **Representative**: e.g. of every significant ecosystem type in a country or region. The conservation of biodiversity can only be achieved if together the MPAs include examples of all ecosystems and species.

■ **Principles of the World Conservation Strategy (WCS)**. Although a little dated now, the WCS (1980) is still the most cogent and accessible account of how to fuse conservation and development objectives (see Foreword).

How has marine conservation been approached up to now?

To date, there have been three principal approaches to marine conservation:

1. Specialist agencies regulated and managed individual marine activities, such as commercial fishing, with varying degrees of coordination. Usually there was little or no coordination with the management of adjacent coastal lands. This included protection of individual species, such as the controls on take of whales agreed through the International Whaling Commission.

2. The creation of small marine protected areas, which gave special protection to particularly valuable sites within broad areas subject to more general regulations as under (1), above. This is the most common application of the concept of MPAs.

3. The establishment of large, multiple use protected areas with an integrated management system providing levels of protection that vary throughout the area. Ideally integration should extend to coordinated management of marine and terrestrial areas in the coastal zone and beyond, but in many cases the complexity of jurisdictions and competition between government agencies effectively preclude this.

These guidelines focus on the second and third of these approaches. Both can achieve conservation goals but the second – the network of small areas – will only do so if it is possible, in association with other management actions, to address the key threats to the marine ecosystem. In practice, the necessary integration of management is often not possible. Thus, while small MPAs can be a useful start towards a more integrated system, on their own they may prove an inadequate response to conservation needs.

There is a global debate about the relevant merits of small, highly protected MPAs and large, multiple use MPAs. Much of this dispute arises from the misconception that it must be one or the other. In fact, nearly all large, multiple use MPAs include highly protected zones, which can function in the same way as individual highly protected MPAs. Conversely, a small, highly protected MPA in a larger area subject to integrated management can be as effective in conservation terms as a large, multiple use MPA.

What progress has been made in creating MPAs?

MPAs have existed for hundreds of years. In the Pacific, for example, there were many areas where extractive use was prohibited by community leaders so as to allow regeneration of the resources.

However, most statutory MPAs are very recent. In 1970, only 118 were known; by 1985, only 430. By 1994, there were some 1306 MPAs, but over half were in four marine regions – the Wider Caribbean, the Northeast Pacific, the Northwest Pacific and

Australia/New Zealand. Moreover, these figures exclude MPAs which were established voluntarily rather than by statute, and protected areas that are predominantly terrestrial but include some marine components.

Progress may be encouraging but there is still much to be done. While less than 1% of the marine environment is currently within protected areas, the comparable figure on land is nearly 9%.

Moreover, many MPAs are under threat. In 1995, the World Resources Institute estimated that over half of MPAs were at high risk from nearby intensive coastal development. Furthermore, MPAs are often established but then an effective management system is not put in place. In most regions, MPAs with effective management are outnumbered by those with ineffective management or none at all. "Paper parks" are probably more common in the marine environment than on land, in part because marking boundaries is difficult. This is particularly true of many fisheries reserves where the intended controls on fishing are often not followed. Users often claim, "I didn't know I was in a protected area!".

Lack of integrated coastal management is a major problem in most countries and for most MPAs. If pollution and erosion from land that reaches the sea are not controlled, protective action in the marine environment may be futile. The only effective conservation course is to control the pollution and erosion at source. However, in many countries, the institutional coordination mechanisms to address these multiple threats are lacking. For example, the institution in charge of coastal marine management may be the Department of Fisheries, which rarely has a mandate to address pollution.

What has IUCN contributed to MPAs?

IUCN's contribution to MPAs dates back to the 1970s when a few dedicated individuals started to develop programmes to establish MPAs in various parts of the world and to develop the basic concept of an MPA. IUCN has long had a Marine Conservation Programme, and today most of its Regional and Country Offices support various marine conservation activities. WCPA (formerly CNPPA) has had a marine wing since it created the post of Vice-Chair (Marine) in 1986. The Vice-Chair has set up and coordinates 18 groups of volunteer specialists, each covering a coastal marine region and a further group working on issues of the High Seas.

Particular activities include:

- In 1975, an IUCN conference in Tokyo called for the establishment of a well-monitored system of MPAs representative of the world's marine ecosystems.

- In 1982, CNPPA organized a series of workshops on the creation and management of marine and coastal protected areas, as part of the 3rd World Congress on National Parks (Bali, Indonesia). This led to the publication of *Marine and Coastal Protected Areas: A Guide for Planners and Managers* (the 'Orange Book' – Salm and Clark, 1984), which provides a detailed guide on how to manage marine and coastal protected areas.

- In 1991, IUCN published *Guidelines for Establishing Marine Protected Areas*, which are comprehensively revised in this edition.

■ In 1992, at the 4ᵗʰWorld Congress on Protected Areas (Caracas, Venezuela), a Caracas Action Plan was adopted – see Box 3 – which is relevant in a number of significant ways to MPAs.

■ In 1995, the landmark report, *A Global Representative System of Marine Protected Areas* was published in four volumes. Undertaken by CNPPA jointly with The Great Barrier Reef Marine Park Authority (Australia) and the World Bank, this detailed report sets out the situation in each of the 18 marine regions and outlines what further MPAs are needed. It has led, among many other actions, to demonstration projects to establish multiple use MPAs in Samoa, Tanzania and Vietnam, with World Bank/GEF funding.

How were the previous guidelines received?

IUCN circulated the previous 1991 version of the Guidelines to many potential users around the world. They were translated into various languages and contributed to a rapid expansion of activity to establish MPAs around the world. Most notably, the

---

Box 3   Recent trends in protected area management

The IVth World Parks Congress in Caracas, Venezuela (1992) set out a number of objectives and high priority actions for protected areas worldwide in the Caracas Action Plan. Since 1992, increasing emphasis has been given to:

■ Bioregional planning, as an integrated approach to link protected area management to the use of land and water in the surrounding landscape. This is essentially a similar approach to integrated coastal management and emphasizes the links between terrestrial and marine environments.

■ Co-management, which encourages good relations with the local community and their active involvement in the planning and management of the area. It is proving an ideal way of involving fishers and other stakeholders in MPA management.

■ The changing structure of management. The trend has been for more private sector, local community, indigenous peoples and NGO involvement in the management of protected areas, following devolution of government functions as part of democratization and other trends. Not so well developed as on land, this trend is only just starting in the seas.

■ Financial sustainability. The need is for protected areas to be more financially self-sustaining, by generating their own income and not relying on government budgets as their only source of funding. This depends on governments allowing MPA managers to retain the income they have generated for management, a practice which finance departments sometimes oppose.

■ The use of protected area models in which people work and live, as a way of combining conservation of biodiversity with continuation of local livelihoods and services. As a result, protected areas in Category V (protected lived-in landscapes) and Category VI (sustainable use reserves) are increasingly used.

Asian members of WCPA adopted them at their Beijing conference in 1994, deciding to follow the guidelines and to develop a system of MPAs in their region.

The selection criteria have been adopted in other regions and circumstances. For example they have been used by the International Maritime Organisation (IMO) and were integrated into the Principles and Guidelines for Site Selection for the Circumpolar Protected Area Network (CPAN) being implemented by the eight Arctic countries of the Arctic Council.

It is indeed gratifying that the pace of MPA establishment has accelerated rapidly in the 1990s and continues to do so. The Guidelines have contributed to this welcome development. But there is still so much to do and so much to catch up!

1. Placing Marine Protected Areas in their wider context

1.1 MPAs are essential for marine conservation. However, the seas will only be conserved effectively by integrated management regimes that deal with all the human activities that affect marine life

Acid rain shows the long distance linkages between distant sites on land. Sea-water is about 800 times denser than air, and so has a much greater capacity to suspend, sustain and transport molecules, particles, propagules, plants, animals, pollutants and debris. Sea currents regularly carry the contents of the water column from one part of an ocean to another. Therefore, unless a sea area is very large, it is inappropriate, even for the convenience of research and design, to consider it in isolation. Despite the great length of coastlines and the vast distances of the oceans, marine ecosystems are often closely linked to each other and to activities on land.

For this reason, it is even more important that the creation of marine protected areas is an integral part of overall resource management for conservation and sustainable use than is the case on land. It follows that the successful establishment and management of MPAs depends upon there being an overall framework for resource management, conservation and sustainable use. This may have to extend beyond individual juris-dictions; in some regions such as enclosed seas like the Mediterranean, a framework for international cooperation is essential. Such frameworks will need to embrace the terrestrial and the marine environments.

1.2 The establishment of an MPA should be integrated with other policies for use of land and sea

Various approaches have emerged to deliver conservation and development effect-ively, such as bioregional planning, integrated coastal management and integrated ecosystem management. Recently, IUCN has proposed the concept of Ecosystem Management (EM) as the overarching approach. All these approaches have two fundamental features in common:

a) They cover a large area;

b) They take an ecosystem-based approach, which treats the land and the sea as a single integrated system.

The value of the MPA can be completely jeopardized if pollution from land-based sources cannot be controlled. Yet few MPA managers in the world can claim they have a decisive influence on activities on land. Nevertheless, influencing the management of the nearby land should be a long-term objective of management, and should be

1

considered when the legal status and powers of the MPA are decided. The more influence the MPA manager has on the control of land-based pollution sources, in particular, the more effective the MPA will be. One successful example, the Florida Keys MPA, has significantly affected treatment of waste from adjacent towns.

It is a mistake to try and integrate all the relevant uses and sectors at once. One reason why integrated management is so difficult is that managers have tried to deal with all activities at the same time. The key to success is to be selective and deal with the most important issues first; the others can be addressed as the programme matures, its credibility grows and the public accepts the need for integration.

Ecosystem management is appropriate for localized threats. But if the threats are mobile, such as destructive fishing by outsiders, an ecosystem-based approach will not be enough. A national or international strategy may be needed to address such threats. A good threat analysis is therefore recommended as a key step near the beginning of the planning process.

1.3 Countries should ensure that all the ecosystem types within their area of jurisdiction are represented in their MPA systems

There is a tendency to focus on the nearshore and the territorial waters, which are usually 3–12 nautical miles from the shore. However, all types of habitat on the continental shelf need to be protected for a system of MPAs to be fully representative. Therefore it is important for the MPA to protect marine life to the limits of the Exclusive Economic Zone (EEZ). In EEZs, countries can control fishing, bottom-trawling, mining and other uses. (Under UNCLOS, if a country does not use its resources in its EEZs to sustainable limits, it is obliged to make these resources available to other countries; this could be a powerful incentive to creating MPAs in the EEZ.)

1.4 Regional cooperation may be essential in establishing marine protected areas

Many proposals for MPAs will affect not just one country but their neighbours too. This is the reason why regional cooperation (meaning cooperation between rather than within countries) is so important in marine conservation. In regions like the Caribbean and North Sea, the boundaries of marine ecosystems often cross boundaries of state jurisdiction, so that applying ecosystem management methods will involve more than one country.

As with terrestrial transborder parks, marine protected areas can be effective ways for countries to work together and so can help break down cultural and linguistic barriers between countries.

An important mechanism for regional cooperation in marine conservation is the Regional Seas Programme of the United Nations Environment Programme (UNEP). Action Plans are established with emphasis on protection of marine living resources from pollution and over-exploitation, including MPAs. The first Action Plan was adopted for the Mediterranean in 1975.

There are also other effective examples of bilateral and multilateral cooperation. For example, the South Pacific Regional Environment Programme (SPREP), which is the main vehicle for collaboration on conservation in the Pacific region, encourages community-based conservation areas which extend into the marine environment. Denmark, Germany and Netherlands have collaborated for many years over the conservation of the Wadden Sea, with strong NGO involvement. There is a strong programme for cooperation on marine conservation under the Arctic Council. In the Baltic, the surrounding nations are creating a large network of MPAs under the Helsinki Convention. In 1999, France, Italy and Monaco declared the Ligurian Sea (85,000km^2 of the Mediterranean in the angle between France and Italy) to be a cetacean sanctuary, much of which is in international waters. The Turtle Islands Protected Area was set up jointly by the Philippines and Malaysia. In Africa, Kenya, Tanzania, Mozambique and South Africa are setting up three transboundary MPAs.

The Antarctic is a special case. The 43 Antarctic Treaty nations operate within a regime of cooperation. Specific agreements under the Antarctic Treaty system prohibit mining anywhere on the continent and establish environmental controls on all activities. The exploitation of living resources in the seas around the Antarctic Continent is subject to the provisions of the Convention on the Conservation of Antarctic Marine Living Resources (CCAMLR) as well as pollution prevention measures under the treaty system. The whole of the Southern Ocean is a whale sanctuary under the International Whaling Commission (IWC).

1.5 Utilize recent international agreements for support

In recent years, much decision-making on environmental questions has moved from the national to the international stage, especially where issues have a clear international dimension, such as climate change, migratory birds and use of biodiversity. The management of the sea is clearly such an issue.

International agreements and programmes that could be of particular value to the establishment of MPAs include:

1.5.1 The UN Convention on the Law of the Sea (UNCLOS)

Increasing technical capability to exploit mineral resources on or beneath the sea bed and to exploit fishery resources in deep waters led to the Third United Nations Conference of the Law of the Sea, which ran from 1973 to 1977. The outcome was an agreement to enable nations to take measures, including regulation of fishing and protection of living resources of the continental shelf, to a distance of 200 nautical miles from their national jurisdictional baseline. This provided a legal basis on which MPAs could be established and marine resources conserved in areas beyond territorial seas. Importantly, this convention, which came into force in November 1994, creates a formal responsibility for countries to protect the sea from land-sourced pollution.

1.5.2 The Convention on Biological Diversity (CBD)

Entering into force in December 1993, this framework agreement is for the conservation of biodiversity (which is defined so as to include biological productivity), sustainable use of biological resources and the sharing of benefits from the use of biodiversity. It contains many clauses supporting the case for marine conservation in general and the establishment of MPAs in particular. Countries are obliged, among many other things, to develop national biodiversity strategies, to identify and monitor important components of biodiversity, to establish a system of protected areas to conserve biodiversity, to promote environmentally sound and sustainable development in areas adjacent to protected areas and to rehabilitate and restore degraded ecosystems. This agreement is described in detail in IUCN's *Guide to the Convention on Biological Diversity* (Glowka *et al.*, 1994) to which the reader is referred for more information.

Under the Jakarta Mandate on Marine and Coastal Biological Diversity, adopted by the Parties to the CBD in 1995, Governments affirmed the importance of marine and coastal biodiversity. Five thematic issues were identified for action, including Marine and Coastal Protected Areas. Programme activities were approved in two areas: research and monitoring on the values of marine and coastal protected areas, and the development of criteria for their establishment and management.

1.5.3   The Ramsar or Wetlands Convention

The Convention on Wetlands of International Importance (Ramsar, Iran, 1971) has as its mission, "The conservation and wise use of wetlands by national action and international cooperation as a means of achieving sustainable development throughout the world". Although initially focused on wetlands for migratory waterbirds, the Convention now takes into account the full range of wetland functions and values, and the need for an integrated approach to their management.

A principal obligation of Contracting Parties is to designate sites for the Ramsar List of Wetlands of International Importance. Sites on the List must be managed to avoid changes in their "ecological character". There are currently 116 Contracting Parties and 1005 listed sites (Ramsar Sites) worldwide, the majority at least partially covered by protected area designations at national or sub-national level. Parties are assisted by a Secretariat, the Ramsar Bureau, based in Gland, Switzerland.

Some 48% of the designated Ramsar sites include the coast and so may contain marine components. MPA managers may therefore see a Ramsar designation as an additional form of protection that could be added relatively easily to at least part of their sites. The Conference of Parties of the Convention has urged countries to give priority to designating new sites from wetland types that are currently under-represented on the Ramsar List so far, including coral reefs, mangroves and sea-grass beds.

1.5.4   The World Heritage Convention

The Convention Concerning the Protection of the World Cultural and Natural Heritage, known as the World Heritage Convention, adopted by the UNESCO General Conference in 1972, entered into force in 1975 and now has 158 State Parties. The UNESCO World Heritage Centre provides its Secretariat. The Convention aims to identify and protect cultural and natural sites of outstanding, universal value.

Sites are nominated by governments and, following acceptance by the World Heritage Committee, are inscribed on the World Heritage List, as Natural, Cultural, or Mixed Natural/Cultural Sites. By the end of 1998, the World Heritage List contained a total of 582 sites – 445 Cultural, 117 Natural and 20 Mixed in 114 States. The Convention has proved a powerful lever in preventing damage to listed sites, which can be added to the List of World Heritage in Danger. Some financial assistance is available from the World Heritage Fund, provided by UNESCO's Member States.

The two main marine areas covered so far are the Belize Barrier Reef and the Great Barrier Reef (Australia), though World Heritage sites such as Tubbataha Reef (Philippines), Ujong Kulong (Indonesia), Shark Bay (Australia), Galapagos Islands (Ecuador) and Glacier Bay (Canada) contain large marine components, and others are estuarine, such as Banc d'Arguin (Mauritania) and the Sunderbans (Bangladesh).

1.5.5 The UNESCO Man and the Biosphere Programme and its work on Biosphere Reserves

The concept of the biosphere reserve is of great relevance to MPAs. Indeed, it would be hard to find a significant difference in concept between a biosphere reserve and the large multiple-use MPA.

A UNESCO conference in 1968 conceived the idea of biosphere reserves as places to emphasize the human dimension of conserving and using the resources of the planet. Today, they are defined as "areas of terrestrial and coastal-marine ecosystems which are internationally recognized for promoting and demonstrating a balanced relationship between people and nature".

A biosphere reserve has three functions:

- Conservation, contributing to the conservation of landscapes, ecosystems, species and genetic variation;

- Development, fostering economic development which is ecologically and culturally sustainable;

- Provision of sites and facilities to support research, monitoring, training and education related to local, regional and global conservation and development issues.

The combination of these three functions provides an outcome that is greater than the sum of its parts. This is the special character of the biosphere reserve.

Biosphere reserves are organized into three inter-related zones:

- A **core** area, which should be legally established to ensure long-term protection and which should be large enough to meet defined conservation objectives. There is minimal human activity.

- A **buffer** zone around or next to the core, where activities must be regulated to protect the core zone. This can be an area for research to develop approaches for sustainable use of natural resources in the wider ecosystem in an economically viable way. It is also the area for ecosystem restoration. Education and training, as well as carefully designed tourism and recreation activities, can take place here.

- An outer **transition** area or area of cooperation, whose limits may not be fixed. It is here that local communities, nature conservation agencies, scientists, cultural groups, private enterprises and other stakeholders should agree to work together to manage and develop the area's resources sustainably, for the benefit of people who depend on the area.

Countries nominate individual sites to UNESCO for addition to the World Network of Biosphere Reserves, of which there were some 357 sites by October 1999. A Statutory Framework sets out the rules for governing the functioning of the World Network, but falls short of any legal obligations. However, more important is the innovative concept itself, which has proved of decisive significance in influencing the management of all large protected areas, whether or not inscribed on the UNESCO list.

The objectives of the biosphere reserve scheme are appropriate for marine environments, but few MPAs have been formally established as biosphere reserves and guidelines for marine biosphere reserves are needed. India is presently establishing Asia's first marine biosphere reserve in the Gulf of Mannar. Perhaps the best example of an MPA that meets all the criteria for a cluster biosphere reserve is the Great Barrier Reef Marine Park. This is administered by a single agency and consists of about 120 core areas (totalling in area $16,398km^2$) linked by buffer and transition zones, covering a total area of almost $350,000km^2$.

1.5.6   The Migratory Species or Bonn Convention

The Convention on the Conservation of Migratory Species of Wild Animals (CMS), signed in 1979, is a framework agreement under which groups of governments make Agreements, Memoranda of Understanding and Action Plans to conserve individual migratory species. Agreements that are predominantly marine include those on Seals in the Wadden Sea (1990), Small Cetaceans in the Baltic and North Seas (ASCOBANS, 1991), and Cetaceans in the Mediterranean and Black Seas (ACCOBAMS, 1996). An agreement on Albatrosses in the Southern Hemisphere is in preparation. Although the agreements are predominantly about species management, controlling take, incidental damage and pollution control, they may include the creation of reserves, as in the case of the Wadden Sea seal agreement, which includes a set of seal reserves closed to all activities during the birth and nursing period.

1.6   The international community should provide more and longer-term funding for MPAs because of the economic, social and ecological values of marine conservation

The largest international source of funding for biodiversity conservation is the Global Environment Facility (GEF), administered by the World Bank, UNDP and UNEP. It presently provides about US$100 million annually to marine conservation projects in over 30 countries. Its contribution to MPAs is described in more detail by Hough (1998). Other sources of international funding include the regional development banks, such as the Asian Development Bank (ADB), the UNDP, bilateral aid agencies and international NGOs.

More funding is required, in particular as bilateral support, to assist individual countries to establish MPAs. Moreover, support is needed for work at regional and international level, for which virtually no funding is available at present.

Experience from MPAs also indicates that the time needed to establish sustainable MPAs often exceeds the funding horizon of the donors. Long-term support to national programmes is needed, and this may require a programmatic rather than a project-based approach. International aid should not be seen as a substitute for government support, but should aim to build capacity and support at the local level.

A good basis for funding decisions is the World Bank report prepared by IUCN, the Bank and the Great Barrier Reef Marine Park Authority (see Foreword). This outlines for each marine region the key needs, both in policy and MPA priority terms. As a result of this report, GEF is funding the establishment of three model MPAs, in Samoa, Tanzania and Vietnam. But far more is needed to provide the network of the many hundreds of new and improved MPAs for which the report calls.

1.7 Use emerging international regimes to progress towards MPAs on the High Seas*

There have been few efforts so far to establish MPAs on the High Seas. The scale involved, the dearth of knowledge about marine ecosystems and the challenge of regulation have impeded progress. However, recent developments in marine sciences have led to a greater understanding of the interconnectedness of marine ecological features, vertically as well as horizontally, and their far-reaching scales, and thereby to a better appreciation of the value of offshore and High Seas areas. They contain unique features, such as seamounts, and critical habitats, including essential plankton and krill areas; nursery areas for whales; spawning, nursery, migration routes for pelagic fishes; and geothermal vents and deep trenches rich in biodiversity and minerals. There is a strong case to give extra protection to key areas in this environment. Moreover, recent developments within the framework of UNCLOS, and the conventions associated with it, make it increasingly possible to restrict activities in high seas areas that may undermine marine conservation. Further, consideration of high seas conservation in general and MPAs in particular can be used to encourage international dialogue on wider marine issues.

The growing use of MPAs in territorial waters and in EEZs as a regulatory tool for controlling threats, from land- and ship-based pollution and from over-exploitation of fish stocks, suggests that they may also be useful in the High Seas as human activities intensify in areas beyond national jurisdiction. Such areas would contribute to filling connectivity gaps in the trophic, life history and productivity requirements of species, habitats or ecosystems which occur in the High Seas.

One approach to marine conservation is the identification of Large Marine Eco-systems (LMEs), of which some 51 have been identified around the world. These typically cover about $200,000km^2$, and facilitate integrated research on ecosystem processes and states, upon which management can be based. There have also been several valuable efforts recently to identify important ocean areas for protection (e.g. the Global Representative System of Marine Protected Areas and the WWF Eco-Regions). What is needed now is further work to identify:

- those areas within and beyond national jurisdiction that are vital for species and ecosystem conservation;

- the human activities that threaten them, or are likely to; and

- how relevant international convention(s) can be used to control those threats, as a step towards setting up MPAs (see box 1.1).

* The assistance of Meriwether Wilson in preparing this section is gratefully acknowledged.

Box 1.1   EEZs and the High Seas - the legal framework

UNCLOS defines coastal states as having territorial jurisdiction out to 12 nautical miles (n.m.) (22.22 km) from a coastal baseline and an Exclusive Economic Zone (EEZ) up to 200 n.m. (370.4 km) out. In certain circumstances, the coastal state may exercise exclusive resources jurisdiction to the edge of the continental margin – up to 350 n.m. from the baseline. The remaining areas are known as the High Seas and are considered to be international waters.

Most MPAs have been established within the 12-mile territorial limits, where countries have total sovereignty. These are often the areas of highest marine biodiversity and the areas under greatest threat from land-based sources, fishing and other human activities.

So far only 15 MPAs are known to exist in the EEZs outside territorial waters.

As far as the High Seas are concerned, the International Whaling Commission (IWC) has declared the Indian Ocean and the Southern Ocean as no-take sanctuaries for whales, covering about 100 million km^2, 30% of the world's oceans and mostly in international waters. These are not MPAs as defined by IUCN, since their provisions cover only whaling, but they are valuable steps in species conservation. Similarly, through the conventions governing international shipping developed in the International Maritime Organization (IMO), large areas of the ocean that include high seas have been designated as **Special Areas** where stringent restrictions apply to operational discharges from ships covering, variously, oil, noxious liquid substances, garbage and air pollution; for example in the Mediterranean, Wider Caribbean, and Antarctic Treaty area. IMO is also empowered to identify **Particularly Sensitive Sea Areas** (PSSAs), which are areas which are vulnerable to shipping activities, and, with respect to vessel traffic management, **Areas to be Avoided.**

Some 300 treaties affect the seas. The most important is UNCLOS, which serves as a framework for other conventions applicable to the oceans. UNCLOS requires states to protect rare or fragile ecosystems as well as the habitat of depleted, threatened or endangered species and other forms of marine life from pollution. As to fisheries, UNCLOS provides for the establishment of areas closed to fishing in order to conserve fish stocks, and such provisions are found in many of the regional fishery conventions. The UN Agreement on Straddling Fish Stocks and Highly Migratory Fish Stocks (1995, but, as of 1999, not yet in force) goes further than UNCLOS in specifying measures to conserve critical species and habitats. These provisions may be further developed to upgrade regional fishery agreements. A further provision of UNCLOS allows the International Seabed Authority (ISBA), to protect the marine environment from minerals extraction activities taking place in the deep seabed beyond national jurisdiction; ISBA may disallow areas for exploitation where there is a risk of substantial harm to the marine environment.

1.8 MPAs will only succeed if backed by the public, so raising awareness about marine conservation needs is a vital prerequisite for success

Strong public awareness strengthens the MPA manager's hand. Without it, he or she will be unlikely to get the necessary legislation approved in the first place or secure an adequate budget allocation for planning, establishment and management of the MPA. Public support will, however, be ephemeral unless the MPA manager develops and maintains a reputation for integrity.

A priority is to build public support for the principle of conserving the marine environment. Proponents in developed and developing countries should appeal to both the environmental and the economic benefits.

Support from people in neighbouring areas is especially important. This is made easier by devolving some aspects of MPA management from central government to regional or local communities. Chapter 4 and Annex 1 deal with the vital subject of community and stakeholder participation in an MPA.

2. Developing the legal framework*

For most countries a broad, integrated approach to conservation and management of marine resources is a new endeavour which is not adequately provided for in existing legislation. Thus, before an MPA can be established, it may be necessary to review and revise existing legislation and/or develop new legislation.

There are several different approaches, ranging from new, specific-purpose legislation to continued use of existing legislation with relatively minor modifications. In many cases, MPAs have been established under fisheries legislation and, in others, under forestry legislation. In any country, the right approach requires a detailed understanding of that country's culture, tradition and legal processes. There are, however, several general principles which should be followed and which form the subject of this chapter.

Before legislation is proposed, MPA planners need to decide whether to advocate a large number of small MPAs with a regime of environmental management operating in their surroundings or a few large multiple-use MPAs. This choice, discussed in more detail elsewhere, naturally affects most of the issues in this chapter. Perhaps the commonest mistake in establishing new MPAs is to make legislation for small MPAs without the complementary controls for the wider environment around them.

A second fundamental question is whether the national law should provide a detailed framework of administrative aspects or only the broad basis for a management regime. Sometimes, powerful local interests in an area favour short-term economic benefits, leading to strong local pressure for over-exploitation of resources. In other cases, the local community will favour the sustainable use and protection of marine resources. Therefore, the law should protect management from unreasonable local pressures by including a sufficiently detailed statement specifying clear objectives and a process for achieving them. Any detail added to the law should be carefully considered because inevitably it will limit the management's flexibility in addressing the unexpected.

Because the enactment process for a new comprehensive law specifically for marine protected areas may require years, it is important to make use of existing legislation or other instruments (e.g. executive decrees) to begin the process in the short term, even if these approaches are not suitable over the long-term. Simultaneously work can begin both on-the-ground to safeguard the conservation integrity of important sites and with the drafting process for a new law. If the conservation work proceeds well, it is likely the community will become involved and more aware of the long-term benefits, improving the climate for the new law and informing its content along the way. The law is an important means of promoting national policy, but the lack of a new

---

* This chapter is based largely upon a chapter entitled "Review of Legislation" by G. Kelleher and B. Lausche in the *Coral Reef Management Handbook* (UNESCO, 1984).

11

comprehensive law should never be allowed to delay action where irreversible damage to a critical MPA proposed site is at stake. Conservation managers should therefore be alert to additional, complementary or alternative measures – such as fisheries permits, tourism regulations, commercial licences, or direct inter-governmental negotiations – which might be tapped to minimize long-term harm where a near-term conflict needs attention.

Whatever law is chosen, simple regulations work best. Many national regulations are so complex that they confuse the beneficiaries. In general, the **simpler the national rules, the more likely it is that they will be followed at the local level**. Specific MPA rules should be as simple and clear as possible. A strict no-fishing rule inside MPAs is much easier to understand than "prohibition of fishing between May and June, between the high water mark and 1 mile from the shore".

In establishing an MPA, the following should be specified, whether in umbrella legislation or in site-specific legislation:

a) Objectives;

b) Management rules and penalties applied (with any special rules and administrative measures that may be needed, and safeguards to ensure and enhance compliance by Government, including transparency of decision-making and provision for NGOs);

c) Delineation of boundaries;

d) Providing adequate statements of authority, precedence and procedures;

e) Advisory and consultation processes ;

f) Criteria for decision-making;

g) Relationship with other national and local authorities, and procedures for coordination and conflict resolution;

h) Management plans, zoning and regulation;

i) Monitoring and review; and

j) Compensation.

Detailed consideration of these matters is included in 2.11 and Box 2.1, below.

2.1   If the approach of very large MPAs is chosen, decide whether each MPA will be created by a separate legal instrument or whether to create umbrella legislation for MPAs in general

Most countries make umbrella legislation for MPAs, but if the area to be protected is very large and distinctive, it may be appropriate to make it the subject of specific legislation. A good example is the Great Barrier Reef Marine Park Act in Australia, which established the world's largest MPA and set up an Authority to run it. A feature as important as the Great Barrier Reef deserved legislation of its own. Separate legislation for an MPA may be harder to enact politically than umbrella legislation, requiring its advocates to show that the issues and objectives are significantly different from those of other MPAs, but it has advantages in that the legislation is tightly tied to the individual site.

It is strongly recommended that legislation be based upon sustainable multiple use managed areas (e.g. the Biosphere Reserve concept), as opposed to isolated highly protected pockets in an area that is otherwise unmanaged or subject only to piecemeal regulation or industry-specific rules (e.g. relating to fishing). However, it is recognized that the latter scenario can often be the foundation for the subsequent development of integrated management regimes.

The advantage of umbrella legislation for a country's entire MPA system is that it allows principles to be established for all MPAs, with flexible arrangements for implementation by the executive. The decision whether to create umbrella legislation may depend on the types of threats: if they are mobile, only national legislation may be effective. Such a policy should also give effect to the requirements of the CBD and UNCLOS, as well as to the country's other international obligations.

In designing umbrella legislation the following objectives merit consideration:

■ Provide for conservation management regimes over as large areas as practicable;

■ Provide several levels of access, such as strict protection, fishing and collecting in different zones;

■ Provide for the continuing, sustainable harvesting of food and materials over most of the country's marine areas; and

■ Address national legislative and juridical loopholes that allow destructive practices to continue.

2.2 If the approach of a network of small MPAs is chosen, consider establishing them on the basis of community action, supported by legislation

Here, the experience of Samoa and the Philippines is relevant. In Samoa, a Fisheries Act allows for the recognition of community by-laws, provided that they are compatible with national legislation. Once the community leaders choose to establish an MPA, a meeting is held with national fisheries officers to decide whether local management rules are compatible with the national act. When this is established, the local rules are enacted as by-laws, and disseminated to adjacent villages through the radio and by community meetings.

A World Bank study showed that communities perceived national laws which have been adopted locally as more acceptable than either indigenous ("bottom-up" laws) or national legislation ("top-down" laws). This is a significant finding, and supports the idea that enabling national legislation should be so designed as to 'marry' the merits of national laws with the effectiveness of local rules.

Once the network has been established, experience in Samoa has also shown that the small MPAs can be expanded into large, multiple use MPAs, with specific provisions which benefit local communities.

2.3 Whichever of the above options is chosen, a policy for conservation and management of the marine environment as a whole is needed. This may have to take a legal form

An overall policy on the management, sustainable use and conservation of marine and estuarine areas should be developed for the country as a whole, for regions of the country, where appropriate, and for nationally significant sites.

Ideally such a policy should also address coordination with management of coastal lands. The process of creating the policy, as well as its existence and provisions, will help gain recognition for the importance of conservation and sustainable use of marine and estuarine areas, and the selection and establishment of a system of MPAs. Such a policy is required by the CBD and by UNCLOS (see Chapter 1). It may be established within a national or regional conservation strategy, and would appropriately form part of a national development strategy.

IUCN Resolution 17.38 and 19.46 in Annex 4 can be used as bases from which to develop a country-specific policy statement.

2.4 Make sure that the legislation states explicitly that conservation is the primary objective of MPAs

Conservation should be the primary objective and stated as such in the legislation. If this is not so, and if conservation is not given precedence, the establishment of MPAs may be an empty political gesture. Conservation as defined in the World Conservation Strategy means both conservation of biological diversity and conservation of biological productivity. In other words it includes providing the basis for ecologically sustainable use.

The legislation should therefore tackle the issue of sustainable use, linking it to conservation objectives. Without the cooperation of most users of the sea and coastal environment, especially fishers, neither conservation nor ecologically sustainable use will be achieved. The legislation should overtly recognize the linkage between protection and maintenance of ecological processes and states, and the sustainable use of living resources. It may, for example, assign rights of use to local people, as this as a valuable incentive for participation in management.

For this reason, the legislation may have to include as an objective the development of one or more economic activities, such as tourism and fisheries. In such cases, it is vital that the concept of sustainability be introduced from the beginning, and be treated in a wide sense, so as to cover activities that can be sustained from an economic standpoint as well as ensuring that they do not damage other species, resources and processes. The various clauses on sustainable use in the CBD may be useful in this respect.

Objectives for non-economic activities, such as recreation, education and scientific research, are necessary and may be written into the legislation too. But they should be secondary goals and consistent with the primary objective of conservation.

2.5 Changing the primary objective should be decided only by recourse to the highest body responsible for legislative matters in the country

To change the primary objective of conservation should require a decision at the same level as the decision that established that objective in the first place.

The best control mechanism to prevent erosion of the conservation goal is to set precise objectives that are quantified and measurable. These should be established in subordinate legislation, such as regulations. This will allow for adaptation to the needs of different sites, and permit site-level review of progress.

2.6 Ensure the legal framework is consistent with the nation's traditions

The form and content of legislation should be consistent with the legal, institutional and social practices and values of the peoples governed by the legislation.

The customary or accepted ownership and usage rights of a marine area which is to be managed are critical considerations. There may be public or communal rights as well as private ownership. Customary fishing rights need careful consideration. Legislation should reflect these kinds of situations, which can often form the basis for community support of zoned MPAs.

Where traditional law and management practices are consistent with the goal and objectives of legislation, they should be drawn upon as far as possible. This applies both to the traditional, sometimes unwritten, laws of native peoples and to the more recent traditions of a country or people. Where such practices conflict with the objective of legislation – as in the case of open access rights to fishing – education and enforcement will be necessary to change current practice.

2.7 The legislation should take an international perspective

The young of many marine animals, and their food, as well as plant seeds, propagules and pollutants, are transported in the water column, often over distances so great that they cover the territorial waters of several countries. Many marine species, such as the great whales, turtles, sea birds and some fish, migrate over great distances. Legislation and policy should therefore be shaped by and support regional, international and other multilateral treaties or obligations designed to protect these. Such an approach should ensure that the management initiatives of one country are not prejudiced by the actions of others.

The obligations of international treaties such as UNCLOS and CBD (Chapter 1) are pertinent here.

2.8 The legislation should create the legal foundation for the institutions that will establish and manage the MPAs

Legislation should identify and establish institutional mechanisms. It should also establish specific responsibility, accountability and capacity for the management of MPAs. This is needed to ensure that the basic goal, objectives and purposes can be realised. Legislation should provide a general responsibility to ensure that government agencies work with local government and administration, traditional village community bodies, individual citizens, clubs and other associations with compatible goals, objectives and responsibilities.

If management is to succeed, inter-agency disputes, concerns, obstruction or delay must be minimized. It follows that legislation and management arrangements should grow from existing institutions unless there is overwhelming public and political support for completely new administrative agencies. Therefore:

- Avoid unnecessary conflict with existing legislation and administration;

- Where conflict with other legislation and administration is inevitable, define reconciliation procedures and if possible which piece of legislation takes precedence over others;

- Interfere with existing sustainable uses as little as practicable; and

- Use existing staff and technical resources wherever practicable.

The choice of ministry or agency to be responsible for MPAs is crucial. The national parks or protected areas agency may be the natural choice, but if it does not have experience in marine matters or has limited ability to influence government policy, little may be achieved.

2.9 The legislation should address directly the coordination and linkage with other bodies, especially in the management of the coast and of fishing rights

The legislation should provide for coordination of planning and management by all relevant agencies with statutory responsibilities affecting the MPA, whether the responsibilities apply within the MPA or outside it, with the aim of firmly anchoring the MPA in the broader context of coastal planning. Provision should be made to define the relative precedence of the various pieces of legislation which may apply to such areas.

The agency primarily responsible for an MPA should be required by legislation to make agreements with other relevant agencies in relation to matters affecting the MPA.

2.10 Legislation should include provisions to control activities which occur outside an MPA and which may adversely affect features, natural resources or activities within the MPA

Often, low or high water marks are jurisdictional boundaries. Other boundaries exist between MPAs and adjacent marine areas. A collaborative and interactive approach between the governments or agencies with adjacent jurisdictions is essential. The ideal is to have integration of objectives and approaches within a formal system of coastal zone management within each country, with collaboration between countries.

One mechanism for achieving this is to provide in general legislation that all organizations responsible for managing functions that can adversely affect an MPA have as a general duty to contribute to the objectives of the MPA.

UNCLOS makes it a responsibility of every nation to preserve and protect the marine environment in its entirety and to prevent, reduce and control adverse effects from land-based pollution and activities.

2.11   National legislation should have the following attributes:

- Use of terms

- Management and Zoning Plans

- Public participation

- Preliminary research and survey

- Research, monitoring and review

- Compensation

- Financial arrangements

- Regulations

- Enforcement, Incentives and Penalties

- Education and Public Awareness

The scope of national legislation for MPAs is potentially broad and covers much detail. Some of the key attributes for legislation are set out in Box 2.1.

Box 2.1   Attributes of national legislation for MPAs

Use of terms

The definitions and terminology in the legislation should use words which reflect the intentions, goal, objectives and purposes of the legislation and are in language that is clearly understood by those affected. Terminology is likely to differ from country to country but, where practicable, there is some advantage in adhering to standard international terminology.

Management and Zoning Plans (see Chapters 6 and 7 for more information)

For a small MPA, a single series of management provisions may apply uniformly to all parts of the area. For others, particularly multiple use protected areas, a more complex management plan or zoning will be needed to prescribe different management measures in different parts of the protected area. Legislation should require that a management plan be prepared for each managed area and should specify constituent elements and essential considerations to be addressed in developing the plan. Where the multiple use protected area concept is applied, legislation should include the concept of zoning as part of management. The legislation should require zoning arrangements to be described in sufficient detail to provide adequate control of activities and protection of resources. The provisions of zoning plans should override all conflicting legislative provisions, within the constraints of international law.

Public participation (see Chapter 4)

Local users of the marine environment must be involved in the development of legislation and in establishing, maintaining, monitoring and implementing management of MPAs. It is thus highly desirable that public or user participation is anchored in legislation. This should be expressed in terms

---

Box 2.1   Attributes of national legislation for MPAs (cont.)

appropriate to the social situation and in government arrangements relevant to the area in question. The key requirement is that procedures are sufficiently detailed to ensure effective and appropriate public participation. The incentives for administrators to minimize public participation in order to save time and money are real, but it is a universal experience that such savings are likely to be temporary and more than offset by later increased costs.

Accordingly, the public should be given opportunities to participate with the planning or management agency in preparing management and zoning plans for MPAs including: the preparation of the statement of MPA purpose and objectives; the preparation of alternative plan concepts; the preparation of the final plan; and any proposed major changes to the plan.

Legislation should also provide for mechanisms for conflict resolution as well as coordination with other relevant agencies. The legislation should provide the mechanisms and procedures for review of management and/or zoning plans, and may also open the possibility of co-management regimes.

Preliminary research and survey (see Chapter 9)

International experience has shown that it is usually a mistake to postpone, by legislation or otherwise, the establishment and management of MPAs until massive research and survey programmes have been completed. Often, sufficient information already exists to make strategically sound decisions on the boundaries of MPAs and the degree of protection to be provided to zones or areas within them. Postponing such decisions often leads to increased pressure on the areas under consideration and makes the eventual decision more problematic.

Research, monitoring and review (see Chapter 9)

The legislation should provide for:

- Surveillance of use in order to: determine the extent to which users adhere to the provisions of management; monitor the condition of the managed ecosystem and its resources; and measure any changes in user demands.

- Research to assist in development, implementation and assessment of management.

- Periodic review of management and zoning plans in order to incorporate desirable modifications indicated from the results of surveillance, monitoring and research.

The processes of, and the degree of public participation in review of the plan should be the same as for the initial plan development. Provision in legislation for periodic review of management and zoning plans should allow their continued refinement as user demands change and research information becomes available.

Compensation

Experience shows that the success of conservation management programmes depends critically on the support of local people. Therefore, where local rights and practices are firmly established, consideration should be given to arrangements for specific benefits to local inhabitants in terms of employment in management or compensation for lost rights.

Financial arrangements (see Chapter 8)

Financial arrangements for the management of marine areas should be identified in legislation. Provision should be made for revenue arising from marine management to be applied directly to the programme, or to affected local people. This is a difficult but important issue – difficult because finance departments usually oppose such provisions on the grounds that they limit government's flexibility and important because funds from government rarely provide sufficient resources to achieve effective management.

Box 2.1 Attributes of national legislation for MPAs (cont.)

Regulations

Legislation must provide for making regulations to control or, if necessary, prohibit activities. Three types of regulation may be considered:

- Interim regulations to provide protection to an area for which a plan is being developed;

- Regulations to enforce a plan; and

- External regulations to control activities occurring outside a managed area which may adversely affect features, resources or activities within the area.

Enforcement, Incentives and Penalties

To be effective, legislation must be capable of being enforced. This should be through:

- Adequate powers for professional field staff to take effective enforcement action, including pursuit, apprehension, identification, gathering of evidence, confiscation of equipment and evidence, and laying charges in courts of law;

- Provisions, where feasible, for local people to reinforce or provide enforcement; this is especially practicable when local people can continue with their traditional uses of an MPA, even if limitations on that use have to be applied;

- Incentives for self-enforcement of rules and regulations by users;

- Mechanisms for conflict resolution; and

- Effective penalties for breach of regulations.

Provision should be made, where feasible, to give legal standing to civil society organizations and individuals to bring claims for non-compliance and for the judiciary to intervene where they deem necessary to investigate acts that threaten the goals of the MPA system.

Education and Public Awareness

To be effective, management should be supported by education and public awareness measures to ensure that those affected are aware of their rights and responsibilities under the management plan and that the community supports the goal of the legislation. Few if any countries could afford the cost of effective enforcement in the presence of a generally hostile public. Conversely, costs of enforcement can be very low where public support exists. Establishment of the idea that it is "the people's MPA" will generate pride and commitment. It should be made clear in legislation that this is a function of the MPA management body.

3. Working with relevant sectors

It is hard to find an area of coast or sea in which there is not a great deal of interest from various sectors of human activity and in which there is not competition for resources, internalization of profits and externalization of costs. For example, mining the sea-bed creates turbidity and so damages the tourism sector. If a municipality discharges sewage into the sea, it might save the costs of a modern treatment plant but it may affect tourism and fisheries – in effect the municipality is externalizing its costs while internalizing its profits.

Many of the proposals below may sound easy, but experience shows that they are not. Building effective, professional collaboration with the many sectors that interact with the MPA is both the hardest and the most important part of the MPA manager's job.

This chapter is about working with defined sectors. Chapter 4 covers the involvement of the public in the process and the participatory approach that is needed. The two issues are closely linked: cooperation with the sectors will be easier if there is public support for conservation and a general appreciation of the value of, and threats to, the oceans.

3.1 The fundamental criterion for success is to bring in from the beginning every significant sector that will affect, or be affected by, the MPA

The reasons for this are simple. First, if those in a sector like fisheries or tourism are not involved from the beginning, they will be inclined to see the MPA planners and managers as either not interested in their sector or actively trying to disadvantage their interests. Second, no expert, however competent, has the detailed knowledge that would allow him or her to define adequately the interests of most sectors. It is important to bring in each sector **before** creating the first draft of the plan. All should be treated the same. It may be best to work bilaterally at first, meeting with representatives of each sector one by one, but as soon as possible the planner or manager should try to get them all together and work as a team. Only in this way will they start to understand each other.

Dialogue should be not just head to head but at all levels of the respective agencies. Planners and managers have to be able to communicate meaningfully even with people who position themselves as opponents of the MPA, and to convert enemies into friends. They need to communicate with other staff and get them to create dialogues too. So communication with other sectors must run through the agency's work at all levels. The most essential attribute of the manager is honesty. If he or she does not earn the trust of the community, failure is almost inevitable.

21

3.2 Assign top priority to cooperation with those responsible for fisheries

Especially in developing countries, fisheries is the sector that is often the main source of livelihood for local communities and the main cause of overexploitation of marine habitats. Even in developed countries, fishing is often either the largest or the second largest income-generating activity in an MPA, after tourism, but is the one where collaboration is more difficult. Fishers may fear that their interests will be harmed by the establishment of the MPA and in some regions it may be hard to shift this thinking. It is often more difficult to show the benefits to fishers from an MPA than it is to the tourism industry. Yet it is also most important: if an MPA fails and has to be abandoned, lack of cooperation with the fisheries sector is often a major reason.

Most marine species produce numerous larvae which disperse to similar habitats with lower populations. The higher fecundity of larger fish within MPAs therefore helps repopulate neighbouring fishing areas. The size of the fish caught adjacent to the MPA will also be larger than it would be otherwise.

The beneficial effect of MPAs on fishing has been demonstrated in various parts of the world: among cases documented by Nowlis and Roberts (1999) was Apo Island, Philippines, where total fish density and species richness had increased by over 400% in the reserve and the fishing grounds after 11 years of protection, with large fish particularly abundant in the fishing grounds near the reserve border.

Most significantly, there is growing evidence that closing part of a fishery can increase the total sustainable catch. The benefits are particularly marked for fisheries that have become degraded by over-fishing, and where closing part of the fisheries entirely should be part of the management strategy to restore the fishery to its full economic potential.

These findings have important implications for the selection of MPAs (see Chapter 5). From a fisheries perspective, it may be just as valid to create MPAs in the most disturbed and damaged marine environments as in the pristine ones richest in bio-diversity and intact ecosystems. This is particularly relevant to:

■ Nursery areas, such as mangroves, sea-grass beds, coral reefs, salt marshes and estuaries. Enough is now known about many fish species to allow identification of nursery areas on habitat grounds;

■ Fish aggregation areas, where fish come together to breed. Many such areas have been wiped out in the past by over-fishing. The ability of fishers to locate and relocate such places using global positioning systems has exceeded that of scientists and managers to identify and protect fish stocks.

There has long been conflict and a lack of cooperation between environmental and fisheries management agencies. This has inhibited progress in establishing and managing MPAs. The implications of closer links with the fisheries sector were explored in the MPA issue of *PARKS* (8(2)). The Editorial argues that MPAs should be designed to serve the objectives of both sustainable use and environmental protection, and makes the following key points:

■ It is no longer possible to divorce the questions of resource use and conservation, because marine natural resources and their living space is now sought by many different users for many different purposes;

■ Most fishery reserves can be regarded as MPAs, thereby building cooperation between fishers and environmentalists.

In many countries fisheries policy has an international dimension. In the European Union, for example, the take allowable from fisheries is decided by the Council of Ministers in Brussels, not by national governments. Around the world, many national sea fisheries jurisdictions are subject to fishing by other nations, under specific agreements, by historic tradition and also by vessels operating illegally. This will affect how an MPA, especially a large one, is integrated into fisheries policy.

3.3 Recognize tourism as a sector that often has much to gain from an MPA and that can generate substantial economic benefits from it

Tourism is often the sector that can produce the greatest commercial added value to an MPA in the long term. Often too it will be the first to benefit from the establishment of the MPA. Therefore, it should be at the heart of the plan for the MPA. Of course, in some areas tourism can be difficult or even impossible to establish, for reasons of climate, access, threat of disease, or due to lack of specific attractions. Here, alternative sources of income for the MPA and local communities may have to be found.

Some key points for MPA managers regarding tourism in MPAs are:

■ Make sure that the economic and employment benefits of tourism accrue mainly to local resource users, so as to give them an incentive to conserve;

■ Act as brokers to bring the tourism industry and local people together, rather than trying to be direct tourism providers;

■ Seek to convince the tourism industry of their dependence on protection of the natural environment;

■ Encourage the industry to develop and adopt codes of environmental practice (many such codes already exist);

■ Use leaders in the tourism industry to maintain peer pressure on would-be renegades;

■ Remember that not all recreational values can be captured in financial terms. While many are not traded in the market place, they can and should be assessed and the results publicized (see IUCN Best Practice Guidelines No. 2, 1998).

3.4 Ensure that aquaculture is regulated so as not to damage the MPA

Fish-farming has great potential economic benefits, often in areas where opportunities for livelihoods are small, especially in Asia. However, if not properly regulated, it could cause great damage to MPAs. There can be severe problems of disease, pollution and accidental release arising from the intensity of production. Some of the diseases of farmed fish may become endemic in wild fish, and as a result an entire wild fishery can become off-limits to fishing for decades.

In general, regulation of aquaculture has lagged behind the growth of the industry. Regulation is usually done by the Fisheries Department, with whom the MPA manager should have close collaboration. It is possible to include aquaculture in Categories V and VI parts of an MPA but only subject to strict management standards. The guiding principle is that aquaculture, whether inside or outside the MPA, should be carried out in such a way that it does not damage the MPA, from the transmission of disease, the release of nutrients or in other ways.

3.5 Consider the rights of indigenous peoples

Indigenous peoples may have legal rights that no one else has. In the Canadian Arctic, land claim legislation protects the rights of Inuit and Inuvialuit people to harvest marine mammals and other species for subsistence purposes; also coastal people have legislative rights to decision-making on MPAs. In Australia, the Aboriginal and Torres Straits Islanders can lawfully catch dugong, which no one else is permitted to do, and they own the sea-bed in certain places. Here and elsewhere, these people should be involved in the establishment of the MPA right from the beginning.

The rights of indigenous peoples may affect tourism. Their traditional rights must be understood and recognized before tourism can be introduced in ways that do not damage local customs and social structures. Local tradition can also contribute to tourism and to the economic welfare of local communities.

The participation of local people, indigenous and otherwise, is discussed in more detail in Chapter 4. The principles governing the relationship between indigenous peoples and protected areas generally are the subject of a separate IUCN/WCPA best practice volume of guidelines to be published soon in this series, and so are not discussed in more detail here.

3.6 Recognize that land-based activities can threaten or destroy MPAs

Many **industrial developments** result in discharges to the sea which damage marine ecosystems. Changing such land-based activities and industries can be a very long term task. Many are economically marginal and cannot afford expensive environmental protection measures, even if these are sometimes beneficial to the industry in the long term. Managers of MPAs which are subject to adverse effects from land activities of this kind can play a vital and productive role in supporting research into problems and their solution, undertaken in partnership with the land-based industry. Since tourism and fisheries can be adversely affected by land-based activities that damage the marine environment, MPA managers should seek the support of these sectors in addressing problematic land-use practices.

Agriculture impacts the seas through release of pollution and suspended sediments as a result of erosion. Such run-off may be the most damaging of all effects of human activity on coral reefs. MPA managers have to work with the farming community to show them the effects of damaging practices. This is a critical element in coastal MPAs and in Integrated Coastal Management.

Changing farming practices is difficult, takes a long time but it can be done. In Queensland, Australia, burning stubble after sugar cane cutting meant the loss of much of the nitrogen and phosphorus and all the ground cover. The resulting soil erosion severely affected the Great Barrier Reef. To combat this, the Great Barrier Reef Marine Park Authority worked with the Queensland Cane Growers Association to convince farmers to mulch rather than burn their stubble. As a result, farmers managed to reduce erosion and nutrient run-off by an order of magnitude, and saved money spent on fertilizers.

There are possible beneficial linkages to aquaculture: high nutrient run-off from agricultural land could be absorbed by fish farms, preventing it from reaching the open seas. In the United States, the fish *Tilapia* is used to remove algae from treated sewage or from agricultural run-off; in China, large volumes of farm nutrients are sequestered in intensive fish farms and recycled as fertilizer.

Logging can be a critical threat to marine areas by causing greatly increased soil erosion. Replanting the forest afterwards will not prevent this erosion for many years: with the sponge effect of the mature forest gone, storms can cause a massively increased run-off that will damage coral reefs. Soil erosion of this kind can also destroy the habitat of species such as salmon which swim up river from the sea to spawn.

Coastal urban development can be a major threat. Many people live by the sea and so coastal development is a major force affecting MPAs. The problems are exacerbated by continually increasing human population. The building of houses, shopping malls, roads, harbours and other structures inevitably results in the loss of natural habitats, above and below water. Salt marshes, mangroves, sand dune habitats and lagoons are among the most threatened environments in the world. All too often expensive buildings are erected too close to the sea and so elaborate and ecologically damaging sea defences have to be erected. Cooperation with municipalities, and especially their planners, is essential. Sewage from coastal settlements is also damaging to marine ecosystems. The record of the destruction of reefs in Kane'eohe Bay in Hawaii after the commencement of discharge of sewage into the Bay, followed by coral recovery when such discharges ceased, exemplifies the problem and the possibility of solutions.

In many countries all three **defence** arms impact the coastal and marine environment. Under the treaty whereby the State of Cyprus was established, the British Navy has the right to bombard an area of pristine habitat on the west coast of the island, in the proposed Akamas National Park. In the past the resulting fires caused great damage to coastal vegetation, but fortunately the British no longer take up this right.

In other cases, the military have proved good guardians of natural environments. Land next to Sydney Harbour, now protected in several national parks, would have been developed and urbanized had it not been under military control in the past. The permanent or even periodic exclusion of fishing from marine areas subject to limited military activity can have ecological benefits.

There are welcome signs in some countries that the military is aware of the great ecological value of many areas it controls and is prepared to work with conservation groups to prevent environmental damage.

3.7 Encourage scientists to use the MPA in their research without damaging its conservation objectives

The science community needs MPAs for research; in most cases, MPA managers will want to help and support researchers. Science can benefit management, by identifying the full complement of species present, by uncovering some of the complexity of how species interact with each other and with their ecosystem. Science, especially of animal behaviour, is the staple of the nature film industry that has done so much to change public thinking on the need for conservation. In short, most scientists make good allies and lobbyists.

Managers should distinguish research that will benefit the objectives of the MPA from that which is neutral. The manager should permit research of both types, as long as it is unlikely to have a significant harmful effect, but should restrict research funded or supported by the MPA authority to the former type. There is much good advice on this topic in *Coordinating Research and Management to Enhance Protected Areas* (Harmon, 1994).

3.8 A range of other sectors will be affected by or will affect the MPA and so should also be involved

Shipping can affect MPAs through the discharge of waste and ballast water, mechanical damage due to groundings (coral reefs are particularly vulnerable), anchoring, construction of infrastructure such as piers and harbour control works and the effect of anti-fouling paint. The involvement of the industry in the planning and management phases of an MPA can help avoid or minimize these effects. The International Maritime Organisation (IMO) can declare an area to be a Particularly Sensitive Sea Area and establish a code of conduct for it. At present only two such areas have been declared – part of the Great Barrier Reef Marine Park and the Sabana-Camaguey Archipelago off the northwest coast of Cuba.

Manganese, oil shale, limestone, silica sand, oil and gas are among resources mined from the sea. Spills, increased turbidity from mining operations and habitat destruction are almost inevitable results from such operations. It is essential that mining authorities and the industry are consulted on proposed or existing MPAs, so as to reduce conflicts and threats to the area.

A WCPA position statement (see Box 3.1) advises that mining should only be permitted in MPAs when it is compatible with the primary objectives of the MPA and should never be permitted in Categories I–IV (see Introduction).

Box 3.1 WCPA Position statement on mining and associated activities in relation to protected areas

Introduction

This position statement is put forward as a global framework statement which recognises that clear rules are easier to understand and defend than ones which depend too much on interpretation. It is considered more appropriate to provide clear global guidance in a statement such as this and leave it to countries to consider what adaptations are needed in local circumstances. This statement defines the position of IUCN's World Commission on Protected Areas (WCPA) towards mining[1] and associated activities in and adjacent to protected areas[2]. WCPA is the world's largest network of protected area professionals with 1,300 members in 140 countries. This position statement acknowledged the increasing application of "best practices" environmental approaches and lower impact technology within the mining industry as well as examples of support for conservation activities. However, WCPA also notes that exploration and extraction of mineral resources can have serious long-term consequences on the environment.

WCPA has developed this position statement based on what it believes to represent best practice in respect of mining and protected areas. The guiding principle adopted in this statement is that any activity within a protected area has to be compatible with the overall objectives of the protected area. For this reason, this statement is based on the IUCN Protected Area Management Categories, which reflect management objectives focused on the protection and maintenance of biodiversity and associated natural and cultural values.

The IUCN category system is being increasingly recognised and applied around the world. A summary of the protected area categories is attached. The position statement relates to protected areas, which are one part of a spectrum of land use. This statement thus needs to be considered in the context of broader efforts on the part of the mining industry, conservation groups, governments and others to promote ecologically sustainable development on the part of the mining industry.

The process for preparing this position statement has involved: (a) preparation of a draft statement; (b) wide circulation of the draft to a range of different stakeholders; (c) consideration of comments and amendments; and (d) review by the IUCN Council before adoption by WCPA.

Position Statement

WCPA (The World Commission on Protected Areas) believes:

1. A comprehensive approach to planning should be adopted where possible to

---

[1] The term mining in this position statement describes all forms of mineral, salt and hydrocarbon extraction

[2] IUCN defines (IUCN 1994) protected area as "an area of land and/or sea especially dedicated to the protection and maintenance of biological diversity, and of natural and associated cultural resources, and managed through legal or other effective means"

Box 3.1   WCPA Position statement on mining and associated activities in relation to protected areas (cont.)

establish an adequate and representative protected area system set within the broader landscape. Assessment should be based on good science including assessments of natural and mineral values. This is particularly relevant to the establishment of new protected areas.

2. Exploration and extraction of mineral resources are incompatible with the purposes of protected areas corresponding to IUCN Protected Area Management Categories I to IV, and should therefore be prohibited by law or other effective means.

3. In Categories V and VI, exploration and minimal and localised extraction is acceptable only where this is compatible with the objectives of the protected area and then only after environmental impact assessment (EIA) and subject to strict operating, monitoring and after use restoration conditions. This should apply "best practice" environmental approaches.

4. Should exploration be permitted in category V and VI, an EIA should be required following such exploration before extraction is permitted. Approval for exploration should not imply automatic approval for extraction.

5. Proposed changes to the boundaries of protected areas, or to their categorisation, to allow operations for the exploration or extraction of mineral resources should be subject to procedures at least as rigorous as those involved in the establishment of the protected area in the first place. There should also be an assessment of the impact of the proposed change on the ability to meet the objectives of the protected area.

6. Exploration and extraction of mineral resources, and associated infrastructure, which are outside of, but negatively affecting the values for which protected areas were established should be subject to EIA procedures which consider, *inter alia*, the immediate and cumulative effects of the activity on the protected area, recommend operating and after use conditions, and ensure that the values of the protected areas are safeguarded.

7. In recognising the important contribution the mining industry can play, opportunities for co-operation and partnership between the mining industry and protected area agencies should be strongly encouraged. Collaboration with the mining industry should focus on securing respect and support for this position statement; broadening the application of best environmental practice for mining activity; and exploring areas of mutual benefit.

4. Making partnerships with communities and other stakeholders*

Involving local communities (and other stakeholders) is essential in MPA management. It is particularly important in the marine environment to collaborate with those using the neighbouring sea areas because of the inter-connected nature of the sea in which actions in one area impinge on another. Partnership with local communities is also justified on grounds of the legitimacy of many community interests in management, such as the use of traditional fishing grounds.

Throughout the world, the need to develop effective management partnerships with local communities is now broadly recognized. This represents a major shift in the prevailing political and intellectual climate in protected area management. Many countries – North and South – have started to translate the rhetoric of participation into practice. In marine sanctuaries such as San Salvador in the Philippines, successful partnerships between national protected area agencies and local communities have developed with the help of project support and NGO assistance. In Scotland, the St. Abbs Head marine reserve is based on a voluntary agreement with significant advisory input from local fishers. In Canada, the management of marine protected species, such as the Beluga whales, is effectively entrusted to collaborative management arrangements with local communities. And in Italy, numerous small islands and archipelagos are acquiring protected status under the impulse and jurisdiction of local administrations.

4.1 Appreciate the full justification for developing management partnerships with local communities and the benefits that these will bring

The benefits of involving local communities and other stakeholders accrue both to the MPA managing agency and to the communities themselves. In particular:

- Management is more effective as it harnesses the knowledge, skills and comparative advantages of the local community;

- The costs of enforcement are reduced, because of voluntary compliance;

- Management responsibilities are shared, lessening the burden of the agency in charge;

---

* This chapter is based on material kindly provided by Grazia Borrini-Feyerabend

■ Alliances between the agency and local stakeholders can fend off resource exploitation from outside interests (which is often the main threat);

■ Trust increases between the MPA agency and local stakeholders, resulting in a greater commitment to implement decisions taken together;

■ The sense of security and stability increases, leading to increased confidence in investments, a long-term perspective in planning, and sustainability in nego-tiated management agreements;

■ Problems and disputes are less likely, due to the increased understanding and knowledge among all concerned of the views and positions of others;

■ Public awareness of conservation issues increases;

■ Integration of conservation efforts with social, economic and cultural concerns for the territories near the MPA becomes easier; and

■ The process contributes towards a more democratic and participatory society.

4.2 Understand the local community/ies that will be affected by the MPA and identify potential partners

The first step is to develop an understanding of the local community and other stakeholders involved. What exactly is the local community? Almost certainly, it will not include all the possible stakeholders in the MPA: some, in fact, possess interests and concerns beyond the tie of locality. What defines a social unit? Is it an admin-istrative border, a sense of cultural identity or an economic inter-dependence? Are communities to be self-defined or defined by outsiders?

These questions do not have single, once-and-for-all answers, but they can be explored. By understanding the nature of the local community, interest groups within it can be identified. This is important, as it is very rare that a community acts as one. Much more often, different stakeholders within a community will have different interests and offer different contributions to the management process. A management partnership has to find ways of respecting such plurality.

In fact, no one body in society possesses **all** the capacities and comparative advant-ages to manage a set of natural resources. Even seemingly homogeneous units (e.g. a village) include a variety of different interests and concerns. What benefits one group, even if it meets conservation objectives, may harm another: the owners of tourist businesses may benefit from a ban on fishing but the local fishers and the processing enterprises may suffer from it, at least in the short term. For this reason accepting a multiplicity of voices and interests in resource management is a prerequisite for fairness and equity. But it poses the question: "Who can determine the values and weights of the respective claims and how can this be done fairly?" Ideally, this happens in the process outlined in Box 4.1: people and groups organize themselves, present their claims, get those claims accepted as valid, and negotiate a fair share of the rights and responsibilities involved. This process may however prove difficult because some groups are politically more powerful than others, while a weak tradition of democracy and freedom of speech in the country may thwart efforts entirely.

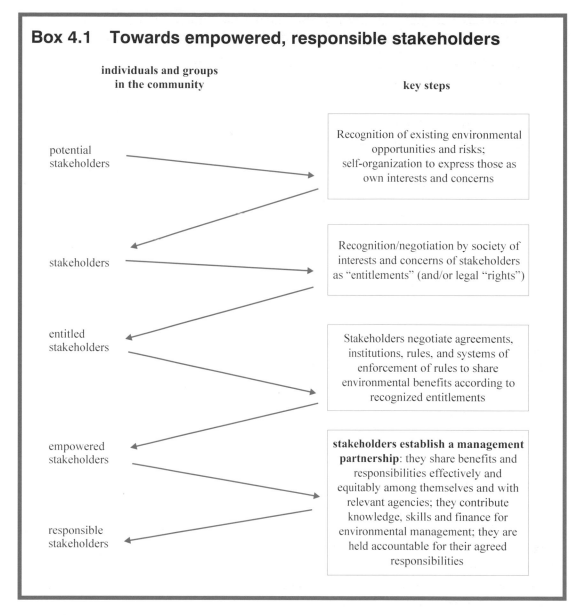

Box 4.1 Towards empowered, responsible stakeholders

individuals and groups
in the community

key steps

potential
stakeholders

Recognition of existing environmental opportunities and risks; self-organization to express those as own interests and concerns

stakeholders

Recognition/negotiation by society of interests and concerns of stakeholders as "entitlements" (and/or legal "rights")

entitled
stakeholders

Stakeholders negotiate agreements, institutions, rules, and systems of enforcement of rules to share environmental benefits according to recognized entitlements

empowered
stakeholders

stakeholders establish a management partnership: they share benefits and responsibilities effectively and equitably among themselves and with relevant agencies; they contribute knowledge, skills and finance for environmental management; they are held accountable for their agreed responsibilities

responsible
stakeholders

4.3 Choose the type of management partnership most suitable to the situation

There are numerous types of management partnership possible. Box 4.2 indicates a range of options on a scale of the least, to the most community involvement.

Only in the local context is it possible to see how far along this path of management partnerships it is appropriate to go. But in general the aim should be to go as far along the path towards partnership (i.e. to the right on the diagram) as is consistent with the achievement of the conservation objectives agreed for the MPA.

Without the support and involvement of local people, the MPA will fail, as has often happened. But without government involvement, the MPA may lose its protection from outside forces (e.g. foreign fishing fleets, as threatened the fledgling MPA in Guinea-Bissau, for example). Thus the ideal is a strong management involvement of local people ("bottom-up"), but also government-driven ("top-down"). Success comes from finding the best balance of these two approaches.

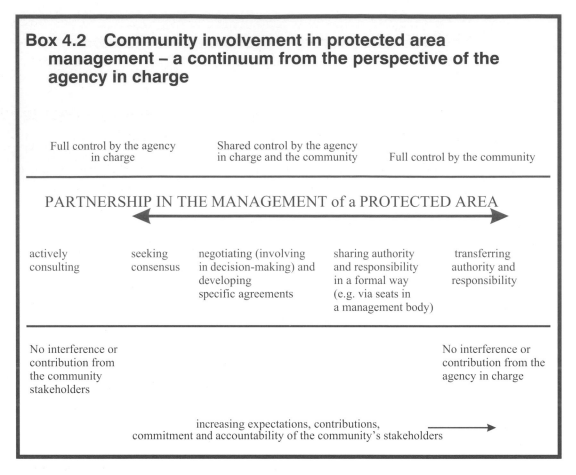

Box 4.2   Community involvement in protected area management – a continuum from the perspective of the agency in charge

Full control by the agency
in charge

Shared control by the agency
in charge and the community

Full control by the community

PARTNERSHIP IN THE MANAGEMENT of a PROTECTED AREA

| actively consulting | seeking consensus | negotiating (involving in decision-making) and developing specific agreements | sharing authority and responsibility in a formal way (e.g. via seats in a management body) | transferring authority and responsibility |

No interference or
contribution from
the community
stakeholders

No interference or
contribution from the
agency in charge

increasing expectations, contributions,
commitment and accountability of the community's stakeholders

4.4   Consider a co-management partnership as one possible model to use

The term 'collaborative management' (co-management) is used to describe a situation in which some or all relevant stakeholders in an MPA, usually the local community, jointly manage the MPA with the conservation agency that has jurisdiction over it. Co-management is a flexible concept because there are many social contexts in which participation in management takes place, with different time scales, actors, processes and results. An open understanding of what a partnership implies allows this variety to be recognized.

Co-management is one option, albeit a very attractive one, on the spectrum of management partnerships (Box 4.3). It is possible to go further, as when for example the conservation agency entirely delegates management of an MPA to the local community or to private enterprise. It is equally possible for a conservation agency to manage the MPA itself, but invite views and opinions from the local community in a friendly and participatory way. Or, more often, co-management may be possible for some sectors but not for others: fishing rights and tourism access in an MPA could be co-managed but control of navigation rights, for example, might have to remain with a government authority.

Co-management is now the subject of growing interest and has many benefits. It legitimizes community involvement and respects the community's need for socio-economic development and use of their traditional rights, while maintaining government interest and concern for the MPA. It is likely to lead to a reduction in management costs, especially of enforcement and monitoring. Most important, perhaps, it is likely to make the MPA far more sustainable in the long term.

A possible model for developing a co-management partnership is given in Annex 2. Box 4.3 summarizes the main elements.

Box 4.3   The elements of a management partnership

The **context** within which a management partnership develops is the policies and laws, the socio-economic environment, the history and culture, the institutions and the rules that make up the relevant social milieu. Obviously, some contexts are better suited to engender and support management partnerships than others. It will naturally depend on many issues. Each situation is unique and the feasibility of a management partnership can be examined only on a case by case basis.

The **process** is the series of events by which the partnership develops and unfolds. In it, various partners recognize one another as entitled stakeholders. They then negotiate, agree upon and implement a share of management functions, benefits and responsibilities associated with the MPA.

The **agreement** (which can be the same as the management or zoning plan) spells out the compromise or consensus reached among the management partners. The agreement is one of the main products of the process, and it is as good – usually – as the process which generated it. In general, it clarifies all the essential elements of management.

Finally, the management **institution** is the system of knowledge, behaviours and organizations (from the least to the most formal) set up to implement the management agreement. Many such effective institutions are practically invisible to the outsider, but they do exist and exert a considerable influence. Others are highly visible and codified (Management Boards, Councils, Committees, Societies and the like).

4.6   Whatever the management partnership, involve stakeholders from the very beginning

Usually ecological or economic considerations are the original reason that a country establishes MPAs, and this often happens without in-depth public consultation and discussion. Too often local people are not even informed on the decision about establishing a marine protected area, let alone involved in managing it, even though the costs of conservation (direct costs and opportunity costs) are disproportionately borne by local people. It is also despite the fact that local people know better than anyone else many of the characteristics of their local environment and are potentially some of the most directly interested stakeholders in protecting it.

It is important that all concerned people receive information on the proposed MPA, not only the stakeholders already in favour of it. Agencies may find it easier to communicate with the social groups likely to benefit from the establishment of an MPA, such as the tourism industry. Fishers and polluting agriculturists are much tougher partners to enlist, but are also the ones who ultimately have to be convinced to change their ways. Indeed, in some countries the initial steps of instituting an MPA are so controversial that some special arrangements to compensate the stakeholders who will bear the costs of conservation need to be arranged. For instance, in the Arcipelago Toscano (Italy), a special fund is being created. This will receive contributions from the stakeholders likely to receive benefits from the MPA so as to compensate stakeholders likely to lose out. This transformation of stakeholders into shareholders is a most interesting mechanism to inject a measure of social equity into the establishment of an MPA.

4.7 Be innovative and creative in the establishment of partnerships

A partnership delivers some of the best results when individuals and groups depart from conventional systems of understanding and behaviour. At the outset, this may require an honestly fresh look at the ecosystem and its relationships with human communities. Some initial investment in research, especially on marine traditional practices and behaviours in resource use, may be valuable (Chapter 9). In some cases, resources may be found to have always been abundant and so do not need specific management, as was the case in the coastal area of Tanga, Tanzania. In other environments, such as many coastal communities in Indonesia and the Pacific, a variety of mechanisms by which people have regulated the use of marine resources may emerge and can be profitably integrated in the MPA management practices.

For instance, in Polynesia, Micronesia and Melanesia resident 'fishery ecologists' – masters of the fishery process – assign permissions to fish to different groups and individuals according to explicit rules. These rules include cultural practices such as avoidance of certain foods, taboos, regulated tenure of fishing areas by specific groups and lineage, various forms of taxation, sharing of catch, opening and closing of fishing seasons on open economic grounds but also on grounds of religion and respect. Severe penalties are imposed on violators. These practices could be incorporated in the management. But others may be negative and counterproductive for both people and the environment. These need to be challenged, even if they belong to the local culture.

Initial research on existing and potential threats to resources may also be very valuable. While a compromise is painstakingly crafted at the local level, powerful economic and political forces may emerge which challenge the achieved agreement. For instance, if conservation in the MPA is effective in restoring marine resources in a particular area, industrial fishers from outside may come in and exploit the newly abundant catch. Problems such as these can be foreseen and prepared for in advance. In fact, external challenges may become a most important element of cohesion in the building of partnerships between governmental agencies and local communities. Obviously, research on existing and potential opportunities – such as conservation incentives and policies – would be equally useful, especially when done in cooperation with interested stakeholders.

4.8 Challenge orthodoxy in institutions

It is often assumed that once elected political representatives are given a role in management (e.g. a seat on a management board), the people who elected them are automatically involved. This is not necessarily the case. For an issue of intense concern to a relative minority, they should be involved directly, not just through elected representatives. In fact, democracy is a governing system in which both delegated representation and directed representation are important and need to be used according to the issue at stake. And all types of democratic processes benefit from an institutional space in which creative democratic experimentation can be pursued. For natural resources management such a space begins to exist at the very moment at which stakeholders are invited to define themselves and allowed to present their views, interests and concerns in an open forum. There will be rules, but those will be developed by the participants, not handed down from above. For instance, the agency in charge of the MPA could help set up an open forum where, at regular times, anyone could introduce and discuss relevant issues. This may constitute an important social sounding box and help identify effective management options and opportunities.

Creativity and democratic experimentation can flourish in several management moments. To begin with, many channels of communication can be tried out. Experiments can also be attempted with the size of management units. Working with different levels of agreements can also be potentially very revealing. For instance, an initial broad statement of agreed principles among all stakeholders for an MPA can be the best platform on which later to develop more detailed rules (this is strongly confirmed by the experience of the Conkuati reserve in Congo Brazzaville). Voluntary codes of practices are also important: 'soft' incentive-based mechanisms are often more effective and respected than hard rules.

4.9 Emphasize flexibility, learning-by-doing and a long-term approach

In a management partnership, it is important not to press for quick results and to strive for these at the expense of building a sustainable management structure. In fact the most important product of the partnership is not a management plan but a tested **management institution**, capable of responding to challenges in a flexible way. If this is understood, expensive technical consultants in charge of preparing glossy plans may become a sight of the past. It is better to facilitate simple but thoroughly discussed agreements than to produce a sophisticated plan to which there is no commitment.

If the management partnership adopts a learning-by-doing approach (sometimes referred to as "adaptive management"), simple agreements are likely to expand in size of areas or resources covered, and in complexity of regulations and arrangements. Learning-by-doing is also likely to evolve towards more ambitious forms of stakeholder participation, for instance from the basic opportunity to vote yes or no in relation to a relatively crude zoning arrangement towards the opportunity to develop finely tuned rules with the concurrence of many people and interest groups.

Last but not least, developing a management partnership implies a large investment of time in social communication, negotiation, conflict management and learning. Because of this, a national agency may be reluctant to embark on such an approach. But a wealth of experience now confirms that it is worth persevering with the establishment of management partnerships. When this is done, often what could not be achieved yesterday can be achieved tomorrow.

5. Selecting the sites for MPAs

As for terrestrial protected areas, selecting the sites for MPAs is a vital task, where mistakes are hard if not impossible to correct later. It calls for good information and skilful judgement. The key steps are outlined below.

5.1 Choosing the location and extent of MPAs involves a different emphasis than with terrestrial protected areas

On land, the concept of habitat critical to the survival of rare or endangered species often plays a decisive role in identifying areas for protection. The size of a distinctive habitat may be small. Despite airborne seeds, spores and pollen and the presence of birds and flying insects, linkages for most land animals are generally relatively short. Consequently endemic species, critically dependent on particular habitat areas, are relatively frequent; there is also a dismal history of extinctions. The case for protection of an area to save a species from extinction is usually powerful and likely to receive public support.

In the sea, habitats are rarely precisely or critically restricted. Survival of a species cannot usually be linked to a specific site. Many free-swimming species have huge ranges. Water currents carry the genetic material of sedentary or territorial species over large distances, often hundreds of kilometres. The same genetic community is likely to occur throughout a large geographic range, occurring wherever substrate and water quality are suitable. As a result endemism is rare and is usually confined to species which brood or care for their young rather than have them dispersed by currents. There are virtually no authenticated records of recent extinctions of completely marine species with planktonic larvae (molluscs, crustaceans and many fish). The concept of a critical habitat for an endangered species is only applicable with marine mammals, sea turtles, seabirds and the occasional endemic species. Therefore, in general the eco-logical case for protection of an area of sea is based less on concepts of critical habitat of endangered species or of extinction threat, and more on the need to protect critical or important habitat of species that are of value for commerce, recreation or for other reasons, or as a particularly good example of a habitat type with the genetic diversity of its communities.

5.2 In selecting sites, the conservation needs should be balanced with the needs of local people, who may depend on the sea for their livelihoods

In most countries, there is a long history of using marine areas close to the coast, often for subsistence. Attempts to exclude these uses from traditional areas may jeopardize the well-being or even survival of the human communities involved. In such cases, opposition will be strong and undermine successful management of these areas if they are ever established.

It is better to create and manage successfully an MPA which may not be ideal in ecological terms, but which achieves the purposes for which it is established, than to labour vainly to create the theoretically 'ideal' MPA. Where there is a choice of ecologically suitable areas, as there often is in the sea, the dominant criteria for selection of MPA locations, boundaries and management systems should be socio-economic. Where there is no choice, ecological criteria should come first.

In general, not enough weight has been given to socio-economic criteria in the selection of MPAs, yet these factors will probably determine whether the MPA flourishes or fails. Because community support is absolutely vital to the success of any MPA, MPAs which contribute to economic activity will be far easier to create and manage than those which do not.

5.3 The ideal arrangement is for a highly protected core area surrounded by a buffer zone. This can be achieved either as a large zoned MPA, or as a set of small MPAs with complementary regulations controlling use of the surrounding areas

As noted elsewhere, the first approach has the advantage that administrative integration is achieved more easily. With the other option, there will be at least two jurisdictions, possibly more, and integration has to be worked for. The MPA manager also has to convince the other administrations of the need for complementary measures in the surrounding zone.

In marine areas, because of the open nature of the system, protection of some communities and fragile habitats may be achieved only by making protected areas large enough that the impacts are buffered or diluted, thus leaving some part of the critical community relatively undisturbed. On the other hand, large MPAs will often be feasible politically only if controlled exploitation of resources is permitted in at least some parts of the area. In general, large MPAs, covering complete marine ecosystems, will allow integrated management regimes to be established which provide explicitly for continued human use and can bring identifiable benefits to local communities. Such uses should of course be allowed only where they are compatible with the protection of the resources for which the MPA was established.

5.4 In the selection process, give great weight to events outside the proposed MPA but which might affect the MPA

As with many protected areas on land, the primary aim of MPAs is to protect the biodiversity and productivity of one or more ecosystems. But because the effects of external influences on the marine environment tend to be insidious rather than obvious, a particularly good knowledge is required of circumstances outside the MPA itself.

Sea currents constantly carry sediments, nutrients, pollutants and organisms through an area, and because of the ability of wind and tide to mix water masses, particularly in continental shelf areas, events originating outside the boundaries of an MPA may affect populations within it. Therefore the minimum viable size of an MPA is likely to be many times larger than that of a terrestrial reserve, unless areas which affect the MPA are managed in a complementary way.

5.5 Choose a biogeographic system that suits the country's needs

Site selection for a representative system of MPAs requires a biogeographic classification system. When choosing conservation sites in the marine environment, it is cheaper and faster to choose sites that represent the various biogeographic units than to use the presence of individual species as the criterion, since biogeography generally accurately predicts the species complement.

Several countries have made significant progress in establishing "national representative systems of Marine Protected Areas" in accordance with IUCN Resolutions G.A. 17.38 and 19.46 (Annex 4). The biogeographic classification system used by a country in developing such a representative system need not be universally applicable. Indeed, if the world were to wait for general scientific agreement on the "best" such classification system, it would probably be a long time before a start was made in establishing many MPAs. The important thing is that the biogeographic system used in a particular country suits that country's existing scientific and information base.

5.6 Have clear objectives before starting the selection process

This is particularly important in MPA selection because of the significance attached to conservation of biodiversity on the one hand and enhancement of productivity on the other. As the balance between these two objectives changes, so the criteria outlined below (5.9) will have to be interpreted and weighted differently.

If conservation of biodiversity is the main objective, the best approach may be to create an MPA in an area not under major threat. Not every marine ecosystem can be protected and resources to create and manage MPAs will always be limited.

If productivity is the main objective, the greatest gain in fish yields may be achieved by closing the most degraded areas to fishing, rather than by protecting the most pristine ones. The resulting MPA will be what is often called a "fisheries reserve", but it will nevertheless contribute to ecosystem integrity and conservation of biodiversity.

In fact, virtually all MPAs contribute to conservation of both biological diversity and productivity. It is desirable to establish a gradation of types of MPAs with differing emphasis on the two main objectives, rather than two separate types of protected areas.

5.7 Political judgements are an intrinsic part of selection, so that numerical systems that involve weighted criteria can play only a supporting role and may strongly mislead

In recent years, proponents of MPAs have tended to use two types of approach in applying selection criteria:

a) A mechanistic approach, in which a numerical weighting is assigned to each potential site on the basis of pre-determined criteria;

b) A so-called 'Delphic' approach, where human judgement is used in every aspect of the selection process.

The Delphic approach tends to produce results that are more consistent and more likely to lead to success. This conclusion was supported by the results of a workshop organized by NOAA in Tampa, Florida in 1995. The assumptions made in the Delphic approach can readily be identified, analysed, and if necessary, changed. In contrast, numerical scores mask what are essentially subjective judgements with a misleading aura of objectivity.

5.8 System plans are necessary but should not be used to exclude opportunities for MPA establishment

The term "protected area system plan", as used by IUCN, means a national plan to create a coherent, representative system of protected areas, embracing all major habitat and landscape types (Davey, 1998). System plans are an appropriate response to Article 8(a) of the CBD, which requires countries to establish a system of protected areas, and to IUCN Resolutions 17.38 and 19.46.

When their preparation is based on a participatory process, and takes account of biophysical, social and economic factors, such plans can help in the development of a good network of protected areas, including MPAs. However, in practice, system planning has not always lived up to expectations. It is essential that this systematic approach be complemented with a more opportunistic one which takes advantage of favourable circumstances to establish MPAs that have local and political backing. As has often been found in MPA establishment, timing can be crucial to catch a tide of support.

5.9 Use the following criteria for selecting MPAs

Having done the preparatory work, the selection process can begin. Box 5.1 identifies factors or criteria which can be used in deciding whether an area should be included in an MPA, and in determining the boundaries of an MPA.

Box 5.1 Criteria for selecting MPAs

Biogeographic criteria

- Presence of rare biogeographic qualities or representative of a biogeographic "type" or types
- Existence of unique or unusual geological features

Ecological criteria

- Ecological processes or life-support systems (e.g. as a source for larvae for downstream areas)
- Integrity, or the degree to which the area, either alone or in association with other protected areas, encompasses a complete ecosystem
- The variety of habitats
- Presence of habitat for rare or endangered species

Box 5.1   Criteria for selecting MPAs (cont.)

- Presence of nursery or juvenile areas
- Presence of feeding, breeding or rest areas
- Existence of rare or unique habitat for any species
- Degree of genetic diversity within species

Naturalness

- Extent to which the area has been protected from, or has not been subject to, human-induced change

Economic importance

- Existing or potential economic contribution due to protection (e.g. protection of an area for recreation, subsistence, use by traditional inhabitants, appreciation by tourists and others, or as a refuge nursery area or source of economically important species)

Social importance

- Existing or potential value to local, national or international communities because of its heritage, historical, cultural, traditional, aesthetic, educational or recreational qualities

Scientific importance

- Value for research and monitoring

International or national significance

- Existence of any national or international designation
- Potential for listing on a national or international system

Practicality or feasibility

- Degree of insulation from external destructive influences
- Social and political acceptability, degree of community support
- Accessibility for education, tourism, recreation
- Compatibility with existing uses, particularly by locals
- Ease of management or compatibility with existing management regimes

Duality or Replication

MPAs, particularly when small, can be subject to devastating destructive influences, either from humans or from nature, such as cyclones on coral reefs. It is therefore desirable that there should be more than one sample of every major ecosystem type in a representative system.

6. Planning and managing MPAs

This chapter provides general guidance on the complex process of actually planning and managing an MPA. Three topics are of such importance, though, that they have each been dedicated a separate chapter: community participation (Chapter 4), zoning (Chapter 7) and financial sustainability (Chapter 8).

The traditional approach to management of marine living resources has been through fisheries legislation. Mechanisms include:

■ Restricting access to a particular stock of fish or invertebrates;

■ Specifying restrictions on equipment such as minimum net mesh, to attempt to limit total fishing effort;

■ Attempting to limit total fish catch;

■ Requiring licences or permits for those entitled to fish a particular stock;

■ Declaring closed seasons; and

■ Defining areas as closed to fishing permanently or for a number of seasons.

Such provisions usually focus on target species. The habitat of the non-target co-inhabitants and competitors of such species is considered only when this is seen as affecting the productivity of the target stock.

MPA management can go beyond conventional fisheries management by providing a comprehensive management package, covering all impacts on the marine area concerned.

The MPAs issue of *PARKS* (8(2)) gives several illuminating case histories with lessons learnt in the planning and management of MPAs.

6.1 Make sure the objectives are absolutely clear before starting the planning process

The purpose of planning and management is to achieve the stated objectives. These should have been set out in legislation (or in formal agreements) and be absolutely clear before starting the planning process (see Chapters 2 and 3). They are **the** standard against which the success of the management plan will be judged, and will help ensure the efficient allocation of scarce resources.

The objectives will determine whether an area can be managed as a single entity, or whether a system of zoning should be used, providing for different activities to occur in specified sub-areas or zones. In most situations, but particularly in multiple use planning, some objectives cannot be applied at the same time to the whole of a significant area of marine habitat. Some sub-objectives are likely to be in conflict in certain situations, and decisions on priority will have to be made. For example, the aim of minimizing the number of zones may be in conflict with that of avoiding unnecessary restrictions on human activity.

6.2 Time and money spent in the planning and development phase will be saved many times over in management later

A commitment to provide the resources of finance, staff and time needed for planning and management should be made at the time when the decision to create the MPA is taken.

Without public support, management costs will rise and effectiveness decline. Without the support of the people directly affected, the MPA will fail to achieve its purposes. Therefore, winning the support of local people is particularly important at the planning stage.

6.3 Build management capacity, especially in the planning phase

Staff are vital to the successful management of MPAs – their training should be a top priority; it should be continuous and include formal training in the workplace.

The management of MPAs is becoming as sophisticated as that of many commercial organizations, requiring not only technical skills but also a high level of managerial and communication ability. Traditional training for protected area staff has tended to focus on specialist areas, such as marine zoology, but this is no longer adequate: today's MPAs need staff from a wide range of backgrounds with many different skills. In particular, communication skills are vital: protected area managers have to be able to "sell" the benefits of the MPA to the local community, visitors and other constituents.

Training can easily be neglected among other pressing management issues. For this reason, the management of each MPA (or set of MPAs) should commit themselves to a training programme that should:

■ Ensure that staff at every level (including volunteers) are well trained initially and that their skills are continually developed and updated;

■ Include formal training in the work place, as well as through external courses;

■ Extend to local people, such as fishers, tourism operators and scientists, who are involved in the MPA;

■ Where possible, include staff exchanges.

A strategy which can provide significant local, national and regional benefits is to establish an MPA as a demonstration or training site, focussing on the training of trainers. Thus lessons learnt can be rapidly transmitted to other MPAs.

6.4 Take a long-term view but be adaptive, review management and do not over-plan

Effective planning and management are directed towards the achievement of objectives. The most efficient ways of achieving these objectives will vary over time, sometimes over quite short time periods. So very detailed long-term planning can be a waste of time and effort. Management itself should be adaptive, meaning that it is periodically reviewed and revised as a result of monitoring. As threats change, knowledge accumulates and the composition of local communities alters, so too should MPA management.

In a large multiple-use MPA, a zoning plan establishes the framework from which the management plan is derived. This means that the zoning plan, rather than the management plan, is the primary document. In a small MPA, the management plan is self-contained and complete. Details on how to prepare a zoning plan and a management plan are given in Annexes 2 and 3.

The legal framework should require a review of conservation arrangements, including zoning, within a specified time. The period between reviews should be neither so short that lack of resources is a problem, nor so long that management is not responsive: 5–7 years is a good time-scale. Review should be based on monitoring of impacts, patterns of use, the effectiveness of the existing management arrangements in attaining the objectives and improved scientific understanding (see Chapter 9).

6.5   Adopt a Systems Approach to planning and management

(Adapted from Dobbin, 1976).

The most suitable means of planning and managing an MPA is what is called "the systems approach", a way of thinking that operates through synthesis. In solving a problem, the approach recognizes the importance of an analysis of separate issues, but stresses a complete view of all the issues or 'systems' that are involved.

The use of systems planning in this sense will improve the achievement of marine conservation objectives. In the words of Peters (quoted in Dobbin, 1976), "Shall we have piecemeal systems based on random components that escalate us toward incompetence? Or shall we have a systems approach that utilizes our total knowledge ... to integrate our social and humanistic goals with our technological achievements and ecological needs? If we choose the latter, man's greatest age of achievement lies ahead."

The principles and methodologies of system planning should be applied also to coastal and ocean zone planning and management projects.

6.6   Bring together an inter-disciplinary project team with clear accountability and defined responsibilities

The sciences are broken into specialized disciplines, but nature is not organized that way. One of the most important ways of pursuing the systems approach is to use an inter-disciplinary project team which pools knowledge and expertise.

In an inter-disciplinary approach, a problem is not disassembled. It is treated as a whole by representation of different disciplines working the solution out together. This synthesizes the knowledge in the sciences, technologies, and humanities. Integration of disciplines yields broader synthesis of methods and knowledge and usually results in better solutions.

The make-up and roles of the team members need careful attention. Who is on the team should depend on the nature of the problem. Marine scientists and ecologists, planners, social scientists, lawyers, engineers and economists are obvious candidates.

Expertise should be available upon demand. It is not always necessary to bring in a huge team, but rather to have them available on short notice when questions arise. A good system of extension services to local communities, backed by a team of experts, may be the optimal approach, at least in support of community-based MPAs.

6.7 Use the well-established principles of project management

Project management is the orchestration of the skills necessary to define the problem and to devise and implement the optimal solution. The basic principles of project management apply to MPAs, whether the planning, design and management process is undertaken by government departments, international agencies, regional authorities, community groups or NGOs (see Box 6.1). The manager should be able to define who does what, when, how and at what cost. This should be clear to all key players.

Scott (quoted in Dobbin, 1976) summarizes the desired characteristics of a **project manager** as "an habitual broad-perspective style of thinking; an orderly mind which can integrate a large number of factors into a harmonious whole; an ability to communicate lucidly and concisely; an ability to get things done quickly; an ability to resolve conflict; an ability to run a meeting effectively since meetings will be the principal communications and decision-making forum."

Box 6.1 Lessons learn from project management

■ Participants function best when they have a broad understanding of the total picture. Time spent in group discussion of problems and solutions will help achieve this broad understanding and build a team.

■ The number of key participants must be kept to a realistic minimum, and their quality to a maximum.

■ The participants should be selected carefully and rationally **after** a detailed preliminary analysis of the MPA, and the skills that are required.

■ The individual(s) who will eventually manage the MPA system or sites should be a key member of the team.

■ The project manager's function is that of integrator, coordinator, communications centre, tactician and consensus-builder.

■ The project should be organized in an organic/adaptive fashion. All aspects should be orchestrated so that decisions follow an orderly progress, and maximum flexibility is retained.

■ Scheduling should concentrate on the broad aspects of key project elements rather than getting bogged down in detail.

■ Cost control should rely on advance development of remedial tactics to stay within budget.

6.8   Establish a clear sequence of decision-making and follow it

The sequence or hierarchy of decision-making in establishing and managing an MPA is:

Stage 1.   Definition of objectives

Stage 2.   Legal establishment of boundaries

Stage 3.   Zoning (for multiple use MPAs) and design of monitoring programme

Stage 4.   Detailed site planning

Stage 5.   Site regulation

Stage 6.   Day-to-day management including monitoring

Stage 7.   Review and revision of management

At each of these stages of decision-making, the following factors should be taken into account:

■ Government policies and MPA objectives

■ Biogeographic classification

■ Physical and biological resources

■ Climate

■ Accessibility

■ History of use

■ Current usage of the MPA and adjacent areas

■ Management issues and policies

■ Management resources including finance

■ Community participation and benefits

It is nearly always a mistake to postpone a decision at one of the early decision-making stages until all the information needed for a later decision-making stage is obtained.

6.9   Remember that nearly all of the management of an MPA consists of managing human activities

Around the world, fishing activity has become more intense and tourism to the coast has grown. Increased leisure time, greater wealth and new technologies have increased the range of leisure activities and the proportion of the marine environment accessible to the tourist. Underwater film and television have removed some of the threat and promoted the fascination of the sea. As a result, demand for access to the sea and informed concern for its conservation have developed from a limited base of traditional users and marine science professionals to the public as a whole. This may give the MPA manager a greater pool of potential support but it certainly gives him or her a greater number and range of users that will need to be consulted and may need to be regulated.

47

Whether the MPA is large or small, multiple use or highly protected, the main ways of controlling human activity, are:

- Establishing area boundaries for specific activities, i.e. zoning (see Chapter 7), including defining no-take areas;

- Enforcing closure during parts of the year critical to the life histories of certain species, or for longer periods;

- Setting size limits, maximum permitted catches and harvest limits on fisheries;

- Prohibiting or limiting destructive practices;

- Issuing permits to control or limit the number of participants engaged in a form of use; and

- Limiting access by setting a carrying capacity which may not be exceeded.

It is also essential to control activities outside the MPA boundaries that may affect the long-term viability of the MPA. Some control can be achieved by creation of contiguous terrestrial protected areas. Local government may have an important role to play in controlling development and other activities in adjacent coastal areas, as a form of integrated coastal management. Environmental Assessment (EA) should be applied to a range of activities, such as large infrastructure developments; plans to increase waste disposal; the development of new fisheries; and proposals to increase the number of tourists visiting an area. EA regulations and procedures do not have to be specific to MPAs: they can be applied equally to developments outside MPAs as well as in them. When activities are prohibited on the basis of an EA, people can generally see why this is necessary.

6.10 Avoid unnecessary conflicts and resolve conflicts which arise

It is vital that community resistance is minimized consistent with meeting the agreed objectives, so do not prohibit or restrict an activity unless this is absolutely necessary to meet the objectives. MPAs are usually in areas where there is competition to use the marine environment. A good approach is to encourage the community itself in defining the restrictive uses. Once this has been agreed at the community level, it is generally complied with.

Nevertheless, this approach has to be balanced against the need, especially in developing countries, to strengthen the capacity for enforcement. A relaxed attitude to the use of the seas has brought problems to many communities as their fisheries are encroached on by illegal operators. A possible motto is "Deal fiercely with powerful interests, but be lenient with the locals."

Plan the means of conflict resolution from the beginning. Conflicts will almost certainly arise, often in unexpected areas. It is best to be prepared with conflict resolution mechanisms and skills well honed beforehand. Managers should also build in the capacity and flexibility to handle emerging and unforeseen issues which may not be covered in the legislation – for example responding to new techniques for fishing.

6.11 Establish mechanisms for community and sector self-enforcement, but reinforce these with formal legal procedures

The "tragedy of the commons" is a shorthand for the problems which arise from unlimited access to common property resources. It is the result of a rational human reaction: "If I don't take this resource, someone else will."

The key to avoiding this situation is the creation of community self-interest in the protection of the resource. Nevertheless, every community has some renegades and people from outside a local area often have no interest in protecting the resources within it. For this reason, it is vital that codes of behaviour in management plans are supported by legislation and adequate human and technical resources to achieve effective enforcement.

6.12 Do not over-emphasize the need for new data. Generally the information required for planning already exists and only needs to be brought together

In practice, most decisions in a management or zoning plan have to be taken with incomplete knowledge and understanding. But before a plan is developed there is usually some opportunity to research and collect information in support of the plan. The realistic aim here is to reduce the uncertainty on which decisions are based, while being prepared to act quickly in cases of political urgency.

Box 6.2 Guidance on data collection

■ **Limit the information used in decision-making to that necessary for the particular level of decision**. Not only can the search for great detail delay decisions, but excessive detail can hinder decision-making by obscuring the major factors.

■ **Use the best tools to arrive at the best decisions**. These include: mapping by hand-drawn and computer methods; aircraft and satellite remote sensing and interpretation; cross-sections and sketches; underwater interpretation; photography and filming: underwater television cameras; sonar; and electronic display screens.

■ **Use, maybe even pay, local people to gather some of the data**. They are on the spot and may be ideally suited to monitor certain trends, such as the arrival of foreign fishing vessels. Getting them to do some of the research may be cost-effective, and is a good way of building their interest, involvement and confidence in the MPA and its management team.

■ **Develop a database for all phases of planning and management**. This may require assembling and consolidating the available information which may be scattered throughout government agencies, institutions and private industries, and in the community itself.

49

In the early stages of planning and management, it is easy to be overwhelmed by the need for data, resources and time to establish a sophisticated data collection programme. However, if time is short and funds are limited, a competent plan can be developed from relatively simple descriptions of the physical, biological and socio-economic characteristics of an area. More sophisticated data add to the confidence of the manager or planner, but they rarely justify a dramatic change of plan. The absence of site-specific information is not normally a good reason for postponing management in favour of more research. Box 6.2 provides guidance on data collection.

Conclusion

This chapter has outlined the general principles and procedures which have been shown to be successful in practice in developing zoning and management plans (for greater detail, see Annexes 2 and 3). They recognize that a plan is likely to be successful only if planning is carried out systematically using a holistic, interdisciplinary approach and supported by most of the users and neighbours of an MPA. Such support will be best generated if those to be affected by a plan are involved from the start in its development and application (see Chapter 4).

Box 6.3   Watchwords for an effective MPA

- Be clear about the objectives;
- Seek local support;
- Build partnerships;
- Plan for financial sustainability;
- Don't prohibit more than necessary;
- Build for the unforeseen;
- Put in place structures for conflict resolution;
- Establish self-enforcement as much as practicable.

---

7. Zoning

To recapitulate (Chapter 6), in a large MPA, the zoning plan establishes the framework for management. It is normally the primary document from which the management plan is derived.

As ecosystem management is more widely applied, zoning will become of greater importance. But while there is much experience in making management plans, far less attention has been given to zoning, even though it is at the heart of the management of a large MPA.

It is not possible to propose a "turn-key" model for zoning which would be appropriate, unmodified, in any country or situation. For example, the sections on public participation depend on factors such as literacy and methods of information distribution. The essential points are that the usage patterns, expectations, attitudes and local knowledge of users should be determined in the planning stage and that planning should not be allowed to become the task of remote experts with no direct contact with or understanding of local issues. However, a possible model, designed for a large, nationally significant MPA with substantial government involvement, is given in Annex 3.

7.1 Zoning is usually the best way of ensuring strict protection of a core zone, or zones, as part of a larger multiple-use protected area

The size of the MPA and the objectives chosen will determine whether an area can be managed as a single entity, or whether a system of zoning should be used, permitting different activities in specified parts or zones of the MPA. In most multiple use areas, there will be objectives which cannot be applied uniformly to the whole MPA.

7.2 If zoning is to be used, it should be enshrined in a zoning plan which should be the foundation for the management plan

A zoning plan is the means by which planners and managers define the purposes for which each part of a protected area may be used. It may be in the form of a legal document but it must be capable of being understood by those whose actions it seeks to control. Planners and managers should encourage public understanding and support for the management objectives of such plans. As outlined in Chapter 4, the key to this lies in appropriate participation of users in the development of the plan.

The format of a zoning plan will depend on its legislative basis and on the procedures of the agencies responsible for the plan. It could be in the form of a locally adopted municipal plan for a small MPA, or a nationally endorsed legal instrument, as required under Australia's Great Barrier Reef Marine Park Act.

Whilst zoning plans may take many forms, they should have clear objectives – see Box 7.1.

Box 7.1   The main objectives of the zoning plan

■ To provide protection for critical or representative habitats, ecosystems and ecological processes;

■ To separate conflicting human activities;

■ To protect the natural and/or cultural qualities of the MPA while allowing a spectrum of reasonable human uses;

■ To reserve suitable areas for particular human uses, while minimizing the effects of those uses on the MPA; and

■ To preserve some areas of the MPA in their natural state undisturbed by humans except for the purposes of scientific research or education.

7.3   The development of a zoning plan involves a number of distinct steps

Ideally, the five stages in the preparation of a zoning plan are as follows:

1. **Initial Information Gathering and Preparation**: The planning agency, perhaps with the assistance of consultants, should assemble and review information on the nature and use of the area; and develop materials for public participation and consultation;

2. **Public Participation or Consultation – Prior to the Preparation of a Plan**: The agency should seek public comment on the accuracy and adequacy of review materials and suggestions for content of the proposed zoning plan;

3. **Preparation of Draft Plan**: The agency should prepare a draft zoning plan and materials explaining the plan for the public or appropriate representatives. Specific objectives should be defined for each zone;

4. **Public Participation or Consultation – Review of Draft Plan**: The agency should seek comment on the published draft plan and explanatory materials; and

5. **Finalization of Plan**: The Government or agency should adopt a revised plan, which takes account of comments and information received in response to the published draft plan.

These five steps are described in detail in Annex 3.

Zoning is one of the most important issues facing most MPAs and is usually the best way to reconcile an array of different uses of an MPA. The maps on the following pages give visual examples. Map 1 shows the zoning system on part of the southern section of the Great Barrier Reef Marine Park, the world's largest marine protected area. Map 2 shows the complex system of protected areas for the Florida Keys National Marine Sanctuary. Map 3 demonstrates the zoning of the Skomer Marine Reserve in Wales; this zoning plan illustrates a small MPA where restrictions on use are intended to be followed voluntarily by the community.

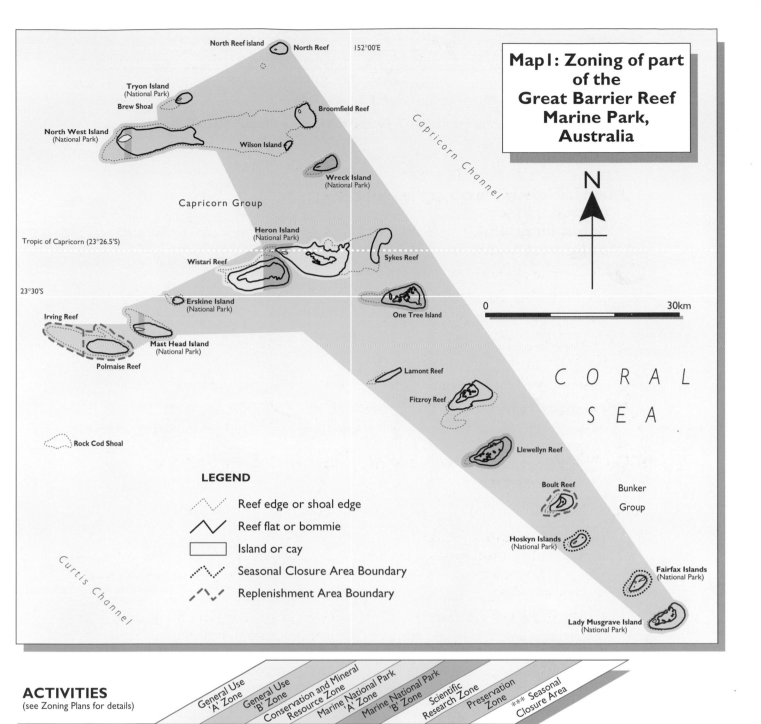

Map1: Zoning of part of the Great Barrier Reef Marine Park, Australia

ACTIVITIES
(see Zoning Plans for details)

Activities	General Use 'A' Zone	General Use 'B' Zone	Conservation and Mineral Resource Zone	Marine National Park 'A' Zone	Marine National Park 'B' Zone	Scientific Research Zone	Preservation Zone	*** Seasonal Closure Area
Bait netting and gathering	Yes	Yes	Yes	Yes	No	No	No	No
Camping	Permit	Permit	Permit	Permit	Permit	No	No	No
Collecting (recreational — not coral)	Limited	Limited	Limited	No	No	No	No	No
Collecting (commercial)	Permit	Permit	Permit	No	No	No	No	No
Commercial netting (see also bait netting)	Yes	Yes	Yes	No	No	No	No	No
Crabbing and oyster gathering	Yes	Yes	Yes	Limited	No	No	No	No
Diving, boating, photography	Yes	Yes	Yes	Yes	No	No	No	No
Line fishing (bottom fishing, trolling etc.)	Yes	Yes	Yes	Limited	No	No	No	No
Research (non-manipulative)	Yes	Yes	Yes	Yes	Yes	Permit	Permit	Permit
Research (manipulative)	Permit	Permit	Permit	Permit	Permit	Permit	Permit	Permit
Spearfishing	Yes	Yes	Yes	No	No	No	No	No
Tourist and education facilities and programs	Permit	Permit	Permit	Permit	Permit	No	No	No
Traditional hunting, fishing and gathering	Permit	Permit	Permit	Permit	No	No	No	No
Trawling	Yes	No	No	No	No	No	No	No
Mineral exploration and mining	*	*	**	No	No	No	No	No

* Mineral exploration and mining are not permitted in the Great Barrier Reef Marine Park. Outside this area, in the General Use Zones of the Queensland Mackay/Capricorn Marine Park, this activity is subject to permit.

** A Conservation and Mineral Resource Zone applies to The Narrows area of the Queensland Mackay/Capricorn Marine Park. The zone allows for exploration and mining of minerals subject to conditions.

*** Applies only when seasonal closure is in operation.

Emergencies:
Access to all zones is allowed in emergencies.

Reproduced courtesy of the Great Barrier Reef Marine Authority.

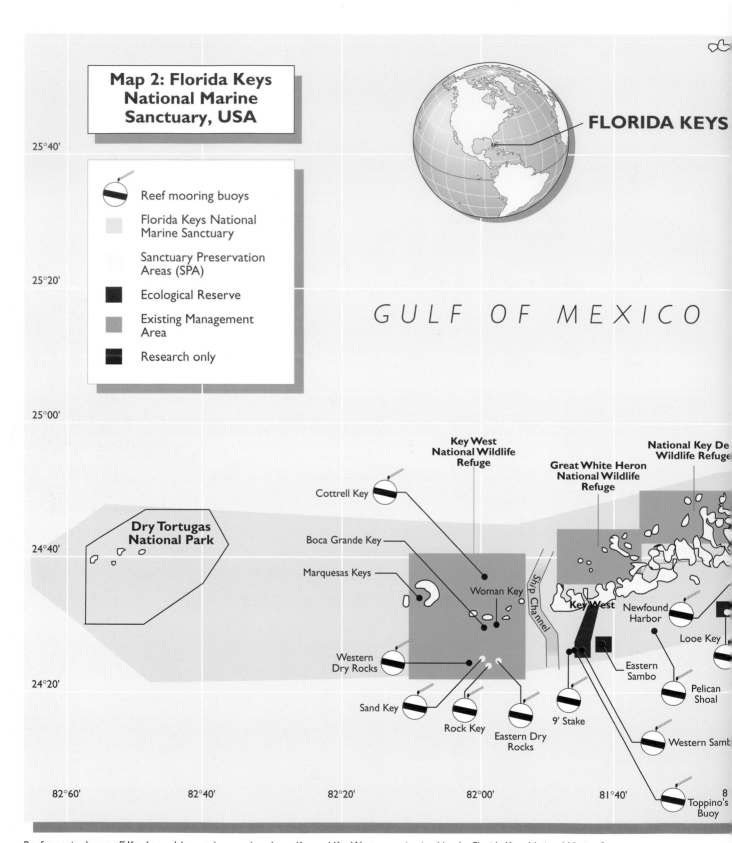

Map 2: Florida Keys National Marine Sanctuary, USA

FLORIDA KEYS

Legend:
- Reef mooring buoys
- Florida Keys National Marine Sanctuary
- Sanctuary Preservation Areas (SPA)
- Ecological Reserve
- Existing Management Area
- Research only

GULF OF MEXICO

25°40'
25°20'
25°00'
24°40'
24°20'

82°60'   82°40'   82°20'   82°00'   81°40'

Dry Tortugas National Park

Key West National Wildlife Refuge

Great White Heron National Wildlife Refuge

National Key De Wildlife Refuge

Cottrell Key
Boca Grande Key
Marquesas Keys
Woman Key
Ship Channel
Key West
Newfound Harbor
Looe Key
Eastern Sambo
Pelican Shoal
Western Sambo
Western Dry Rocks
Sand Key
Rock Key
Eastern Dry Rocks
9' Stake
Toppino's Buoy

Reef mooring buoys off Key Largo, Islamorada, marathon, Looe Key and Key West are maintained by the Florida Keys National Marine Sanctuary; those off Little Torch Key by Little Palm Island, and those at Dry Tortugas by the National Park.

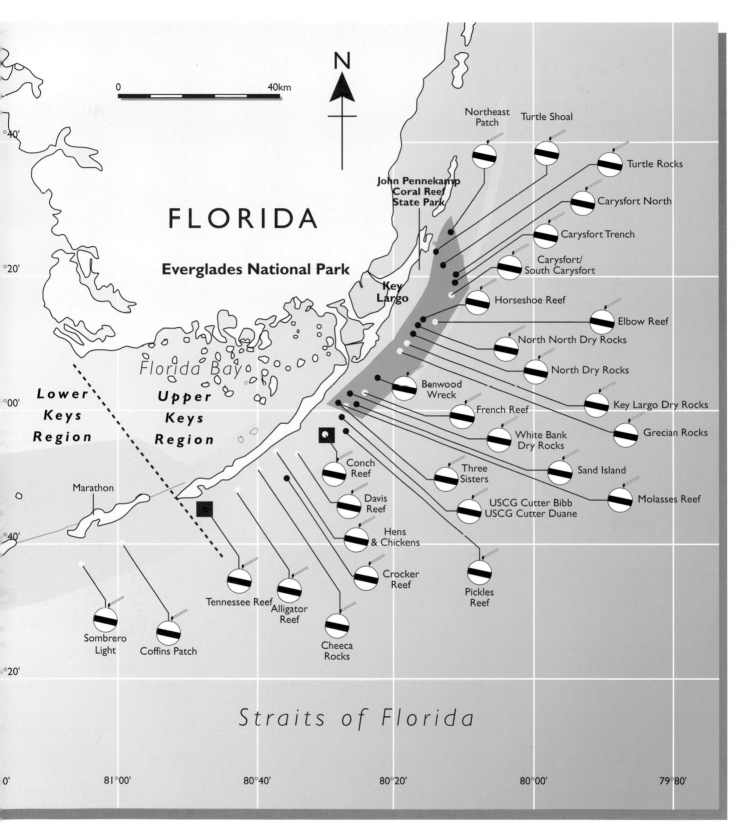

N

0   40km

FLORIDA

Everglades National Park

Florida Bay

Lower
Keys
Region

Upper
Keys
Region

John Pennekamp
Coral Reef
State Park

Key
Largo

Northeast
Patch

Turtle Shoal

Turtle Rocks

Carysfort North

Carysfort Trench

Carysfort/
South Carysfort

Horseshoe Reef

Elbow Reef

North North Dry Rocks

North Dry Rocks

Benwood
Wreck

French Reef

Key Largo Dry Rocks

White Bank
Dry Rocks

Grecian Rocks

Three
Sisters

Sand Island

Conch
Reef

Davis
Reef

Hens
& Chickens

Crocker
Reef

USCG Cutter Bibb
USCG Cutter Duane

Molasses Reef

Marathon

Pickles
Reef

Tennessee Reef

Alligator
Reef

Cheeca
Rocks

Sombrero
Light

Coffins Patch

Straits of Florida

°40'

°20'

°00'

°40'

°20'

81°00'

80°40'

80°20'

80°00'

79°80'

Chart courtesy of Florida Keys National Marine Sanctuary & Reef Relief,
derived from an earlier design by the Center for Marine Conservation

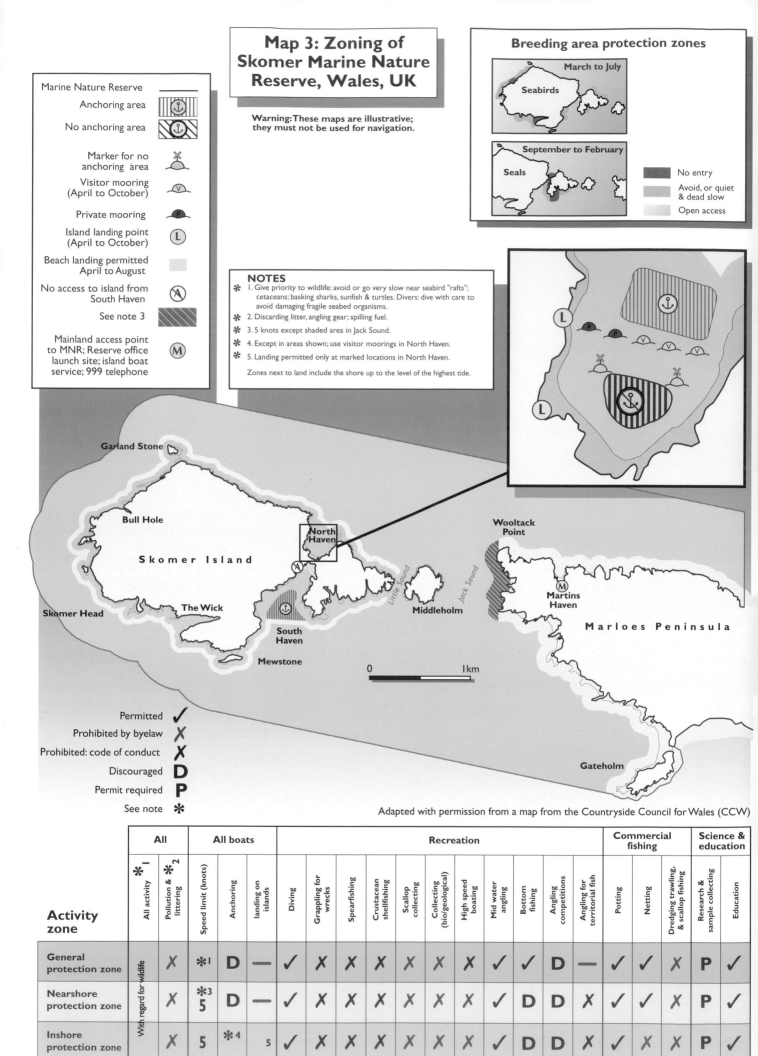

Map 3: Zoning of Skomer Marine Nature Reserve, Wales, UK

Warning: These maps are illustrative; they must not be used for navigation.

Breeding area protection zones

March to July — Seabirds

September to February — Seals

No entry
Avoid, or quiet & dead slow
Open access

Legend

Marine Nature Reserve

Anchoring area

No anchoring area

Marker for no anchoring area

Visitor mooring (April to October)

Private mooring

Island landing point (April to October)

Beach landing permitted April to August

No access to island from South Haven

See note 3

Mainland access point to MNR; Reserve office launch site; island boat service; 999 telephone

NOTES

* 1. Give priority to wildlife: avoid or go very slow near seabird "rafts"; cetaceans; basking sharks, sunfish & turtles. Divers: dive with care to avoid damaging fragile seabed organisms.
* 2. Discarding litter, angling gear; spilling fuel.
* 3. 5 knots except shaded area in Jack Sound.
* 4. Except in areas shown; use visitor moorings in North Haven.
* 5. Landing permitted only at marked locations in North Haven.

Zones next to land include the shore up to the level of the highest tide.

Map labels

Garland Stone

Bull Hole

Skomer Island

North Haven

Skomer Head

The Wick

South Haven

Mewstone

Little Sound

Middleholm

Jack Sound

Wooltack Point

Martins Haven

Marloes Peninsula

Gateholm

0   1km

Adapted with permission from a map from the Countryside Council for Wales (CCW)

Key

✓ Permitted
X Prohibited by byelaw
X Prohibited: code of conduct
D Discouraged
P Permit required
* See note

Activity zone	All		All boats			Recreation											Commercial fishing			Science & education	
	All activity *1	Pollution & littering *2	Speed limit (knots)	Anchoring	landing on islands	Diving	Grappling for wrecks	Spearfishing	Crustacean shellfishing	Scallop collecting	Collecting (bio/geological)	High speed boating	Mid water angling	Bottom fishing	Angling competitions	Angling for territorial fish	Potting	Netting	Dredging trawling, & scallop fishing	Research & sample collecting	Education
General protection zone	With regard for wildlife	X	*1	D	—	✓	X	X	X	X	X	X	✓	D	D	—	✓	✓	X	P	✓
Nearshore protection zone		X	*3 5	D	—	✓	X	X	X	X	X	✓	D	D	X	✓	✓	X	P	✓
Inshore protection zone		X	5	*4	5	✓	X	X	X	X	X	✓	D	D	X	✓	X	X	P	✓

8. Planning for financial sustainability

Lack of funds is a major impediment to the creation and management of MPAs. In developed countries, governments should recognize their obligations to ensure that sufficient resources are provided to achieve the objectives of an MPA. However, in some parts of the world, government budgets for conservation are declining, as a result of economic collapse and a growing population needing schools, hospitals and other essentials. Increasingly the MPA manager will have to generate much of the budget needed.

It is important to separate two elements of costs that may need to be covered:

a) Compensation to local people for benefits foregone by establishment of the MPA;

b) Management costs of the MPA.

The first of these can be very large. It could include compensation to fishers for loss of income from closing fishing grounds. But if the MPA succeeds in generating tourism and in recovering fish stocks, as these guidelines indicate should be the aim, then compensation is not a cost that the MPA management team would have to consider, except perhaps for an initial transition period.

The prospects are most favourable when the communities want to create the MPA and are willing to shoulder some of the short-term costs. This is, of course, only feasible if the decision to create the MPA and enforce rules is taken primarily by the community. In other cases, compensation may be needed.

8.1 Gather comprehensive information on the economic benefits of the MPA to society

The economic benefits of MPAs provide powerful arguments for their establishment. Yet protected area managers frequently say that they lack information, in the language of economics, on the benefits of their sites to society and on the loss to society when natural systems are damaged. More effort is needed to quantify the economic benefits of protected areas and conservation of natural resources. Valuable methodology is described in another publication in this Guidelines series: *Economic Values of Protected Areas – Guidelines for Protected Area Managers* (IUCN, 1998). This recommends that the assessment should involve three basic steps:

- Define the audience;

- Determine the scope of the study;

- Choose the appropriate analytical techniques.

53

It is necessary to identify the audience for the valuation because, for example, the jobs created by an MPA are a benefit in the eyes of the local community, but if paid from central funds they are seen as a cost to the taxpayer.

The valuation on its own is not sufficient: it is just a set of figures. These should therefore be used to design economic and other incentives that will guarantee the protection of the area. There might need to be changes to the tax regime, bringing in charges, or providing grants. It may be just as important to remove "perverse incentives" – incentives that work in the wrong direction – as to craft new and positive incentives. Most nations, for example, still subsidise fishing, resulting in excessive fishing capacity and over-fishing.

8.2 Governments should provide core support to their MPAs

Unless countries view MPA establishment as a priority, the programmes have little chance of being sustainable. International experience indicates that long-term, national funding of MPAs can be efficient at relatively low levels. Such long-term government support provides confidence and is evidence of a serious commitment at the national level.

8.3 Consider greater use of market-based mechanisms

Increasingly, countries are "privatizing" some of the assets of nature, by creating flexible, market-based mechanisms where the rights to use wildlife can be traded. In several countries in Southern Africa, the rights to use large animals sustainably are assigned to local communities or in some cases auctioned, as with some hunting rights. This approach makes the economic values clear to all: it could be considered in the marine environment too.

8.4 Consider the involvement of the private sector and civil society so as to generate additional sources of support

In the past, MPAs have almost all been run as a government service. But this approach is no longer the only appropriate one. Increasingly other institutions and interests are being drawn into the management of MPAs. Examples are:

- Private sector partnerships (e.g. Chumbe Island, Zanzibar, Tanzania);

- NGO-run protected areas (e.g. Bahamas National Trust: Exuma Cays);

- Indigenous Peoples groups (e.g. as in Canada);

- Local government involvement (e.g. the Pembrokeshire Coast National Park, UK);

- Community-based partnerships (e.g. Philippine fishing villages).

Among the many advantages of involving other partners in this way is the opportunity it provides to mobilize resources and tap the energies of different sectors of civil society.

8.5   MPA agencies need the freedom to raise funds in as many ways as possible

The trend is to allow protected area agencies to generate at least part of their own revenue, especially from tourism. Once the agency has raised the money, it should be allowed to keep it. By retaining the funds received, the MPAs can reduce the cost of conservation to the central exchequer. Nevertheless, it may be necessary first to overcome the resistance of the Ministry of Finance to this approach. IUCN will shortly be publishing guidelines in this series on the financing of protected areas. Meanwhile, Box 8.1 contains suggestions for funding sources.

Box 8.1   Some possible ways of funding protected areas

- **Raise revenue from users as far as the market will stand**. This includes fees for divers and leases of moorings and other facilities. Bonaire Marine Park in the Netherlands Antilles is almost entirely funded by visitor fees.

- **Develop alternative sources of income**. One possibility is bioprospecting, using the safeguards of the CBD to ensure revenues return to the protected areas and local communities.

- **Create Environment Funds**. In developing countries, debt renegotiation between States, and between the State and private banks, can lead to the creation of environment funds as a condition of debt forgiveness. These capital funds can be used in perpetuity or for a fixed period. The funds created are usually national in scale rather than specific to a particular protected area.

- **Start a Friends Organization**, to capitalize on the goodwill of the visitors. This can cover nationals, especially business people who want to help the MPA, and overseas visitors who want to maintain links with a place they have enjoyed visiting.

- **Try to capture existence values**, for example by encouraging donations by wealthy visitors to the area.

- **Demand heavy compensation** for uses that cannot be avoided and are damaging to the MPA, for example from pollution caused by passing ships.

- **Press for ecosystem services** provided by the MPA to be charged. This could include a charge for sewage discharge from towns where this affects a nearby MPA.

- **Obtain sponsorship from business**. This is a strong tradition in many developed countries and has potential elsewhere as economies develop. For example, the national wildlife NGOs of East and Central Africa have all had sponsors from local businesses.

8.6   Reducing costs is just as valuable as raising revenue

Ways of doing this include:

- **Co-management**: if local people benefit from the area, they become the allies of management. This can dramatically reduce the cost of guarding the site as local villagers become unpaid volunteer wardens. (See Chapter 4);

■ **Contracting out services** within the MPA to other bodies, for example financial analysis to a local business such as a tour operator;

■ **Leasing out the entire protected area**, perhaps to an NGO or to a tour operator or to a Trust involving local people;

■ **Sharing of staff and resources** between MPAs in a network.

8.7 Donors should extend aid cycles for protected area projects

Development assistance donors have supported a number of MPAs in recent years, yet the results are not always sustainable. The best way to reduce the chance of failure is to minimize the total aid provided, consistent with meeting the objectives, and to extend the length of the aid cycle.

Participation needs time. People may withdraw if the process is pushed too quickly. Even if the final objective is clear, it is hard to predict how long it may take, for example, to set up a fishers' cooperative. Protected areas therefore typically need long periods of funding, though often the total amount needed may be modest in aid budget terms.

Unlike many items of a country's infrastructure, such as telecommunications and airports, protected areas do not normally involve a large capital cost. Buildings are needed, but are not usually a major cost and in most cases should be relatively small and unobtrusive. The equipment required, such as small boats, vehicles, uniforms, computers and radios, tends to have a short life and a high ratio of maintenance to purchase cost. The main cost is usually staff salaries. So heavy expenditure over a short period of 2 or 3 years is likely to be wasteful, unsustainable and raise expectations that cannot be fulfilled. Limited funding, spread over a long time, is far better.

9. Ensuring research, monitoring, evaluation and review*

Effective management of a complex ecosystem under human pressure is not possible without science. The natural sciences are needed to understand the functioning of the ecosystem and the social sciences to understand human-induced problems and how they can be solved. The science done for an MPA has to be driven by management needs.

9.1 First define the objectives of research and monitoring

Research is about understanding the functioning of a system, monitoring is the repeated observation of a phenomenon over time. The goal of the research and monitoring is to enable management to meet the purposes set for the MPA. This then determines the objectives of the research and monitoring.

Research and monitoring should provide answers to the following broad questions:

- What are, or have been, the **pressures** on the system (whether natural, e.g. severe storms, tectonic events or El Niño, or human-induced, such as pollution, habitat destruction or over-exploitation)?

- What is the **state** of the managed system, in particular of its:

  - Dominant biota,

  - Rare, endangered or threatened species,

  - Ecological processes (e.g. sedimentation, absorption of nutrients and toxic elements),

  - Ecological states (e.g. water quality, temperature, suspended sediment levels, nutrient levels)?

- What is, or has been, the effect of the management **response**?

- Are the measures specified in the Management or Zoning Plan being implemented?

- Are people complying with the conditions in the plan?

- Is management meeting its objectives?

---

*Adapted from GESAMP (1996), with input on monitoring from Richard Kenchington and Kathy Walls.

9.2 Next, establish the ambit of research and monitoring

'Ambit' means the topics to be included in research and monitoring, such as testing whether water quality is improving, monitoring changes in fish stocks, and measuring the level of impact from tourists as visitor numbers grow. It also includes the geographic coverage, the time-scale to be covered, and related socio-economic factors.

In defining the ambit, it is advisable to focus on the ecosystem as the unit of study rather than be limited by the boundaries of the MPA itself. Because of the high connectivity in marine systems, there is little value in research and monitoring that is limited to small or medium-sized MPAs. Moreover, the research and monitoring should include those terrestrial and marine areas that significantly affect the MPA.

Socio-economic factors, such as the economic benefits brought by the MPA, can be just as important as biological ones. Indeed, it is often the combination of the two that provides the most valuable information to the manager. For example, if a no-fishing policy is to be reviewed, the manager would need to know the measured changes in fish stocks and the effect on the livelihoods of fishers. It is also important to appreciate the values and needs of the human societies involved, and the capabilities and interests of the institutions that work with the management team. Natural and social scientists should contribute at every stage: the approach should be inter-disciplinary.

The resulting analysis should consider all relevant practices in a given location – typically including fisheries, aquaculture, agriculture, forestry, industry, waste disposal and tourism – in the context of the conservation objectives of the MPA and the needs and aspirations of the communities affected. It should distinguish between issues that are important over the long term (e.g. climate change, population growth and the consumption habits of society) and more immediate concerns, such as those associated with conflicts among user groups.

Table 9.1 contains examples of research and monitoring relevant to particularly common issues – pollution, fishery management and the destruction and restoration of coastal habitats. The guidance in Table 9.1 is suitable for large MPAs covering marine ecosystems or to integrated coastal management.

9.3 Find out what is already known

Once the objectives and ambit of the research and monitoring are decided, the next stage is to plan the detailed programme. First, it is vital to find out what is already known. This may mean sifting through and assessing a large amount of information of variable quality on a wide range of topics, a process that requires skill and judgement. Local scientists can help, especially in evaluating the source and quality of research results, as can other local people. The process should identify any obvious gaps in scientific knowledge, their likely implications for the MPA and the possibilities of filling them within a realistic time and cost.

While each area presents its own challenge, there is a great deal of scientific knowledge relevant to MPAs to build on and borrow from. Often, special research is not necessary to answer management questions – they can be answered by looking at experience elsewhere.

Table 9.1   Examples of research and monitoring for MPAs

Topic	Examples of research	Examples of monitoring
Pollution Contaminant **inputs** (i.e. to control priorities)	Identifying **major sources** (industry, agriculture, fisheries, sewage, shipping, etc) and **pathways** (pipes/sewers, rivers, atmosphere, discards from ships, etc); developing suitable **sampling** and **analytical** methods.	Quantify **loads** of priority contaminants (e.g. heavy metals, nutrients, organochlorines, TBT, oil, faecal coliform bacteria).
Fishery management Stock depletion – causes and solutions	Investigate life-cycles, reproductive features, feeding requirements and habitats of affected species; identify factors (climatic, trophic, human etc) controlling **inter-annual variations** in these characteristics; determine local factors limiting **recruitment**, such as fishing methods and intensity, predation, disease, poor water quality, reduced spawning habitat, etc.	Implement a schedule of measurements to obtain **more reliable data on temporal variations** in key parameters as identified from prior research (e.g. numbers and age-classes of fish or shellfish harvested by different methods, availability of prey species, variations in water and prey quality, rates of habitat loss, incidence of disease).
Conservation of habitats and biodiversity Impacts of development/use of coastal areas and resources	Identify, classify and map **remaining natural (undeveloped) habitats** and compare with any historical records; characterize associated biotic communities and exploitable living resources; evaluate their **inter-dependencies, ecological importance** and **sensitivities** to human activities; identify factors that may determine habitat **sustainability** and appropriate measurable indicators of these factors; quantify relative extents of modified habitats and areas reclaimed for housing, industry, agriculture, aquaculture, forestry, tourism and recreation, transport, harbours and marinas; develop an interactive, computerized database to hold all such records.	Implement a long-term programme to quantify physical, biological and **ecological changes** in habitats with a particular focus on more **sensitive species**, communities and processes; develop indicators of long-term **sustainability** derived from prior research; maintain up-to-date records on rates of physical development and changes in patterns and intensities of human activities; record changes in demography, tourist numbers, aquaculture, fishery production, port traffic, offshore aggregate extraction, sewage and waste generation and other factors that may increase pressures on habitats and resources, or reduce biodiversity.

Sources: GESAMP, 1996

9.4   Design and establish the research and monitoring programme

Without careful design and a systematic approach, volumes of information can be collected at great expense and effort, but these will not enable the critical questions to be answered. Simple and inexpensive technology is often all that is needed. Complex technology often absorbs much time and resources but confers only marginal benefits. Technology should never be applied for its own sake.

The precise design, scale and scope of a monitoring programme depend on the characteristics of the MPA. In many cases, the resources to establish and implement fully the level of research and monitoring identified are not available. The emphasis

should then be on those elements that are most critical to assessing and achieving the objectives of the MPA. It is particularly important to measure changes in the ecology of the MPA, and resulting effects on the socio-economic condition of the human communities that depend on it.

All science funded by the MPA programme should be subject to peer review. It is especially important for competitive proposals to be reviewed before funding decisions are made, so that scientific cooperation is not jeopardized by suspicions of unfairness.

Involving nearby scientific institutions is helpful. Their scientists are likely to be familiar with the historical and social roots of conflicts and may therefore be best able to deal with them. Physical proximity facilitates meetings and joint effort: modern electronic communication has many advantages, but nothing is as effective in solving complex problems as a group of people meeting and working together.

9.5   Establish good relations with the scientific community

Scientists and managers speak different languages, have different perspectives and imperatives, and approach the solution of problems in different ways. Therefore, they have to learn to work together effectively, for instance for posing the questions that management needs answered, but in ways that allow them to be addressed with scientific rigour. The development of mutual understanding will take time. Working as an inter-disciplinary team is the best approach (see Chapter 6).

There will be predictable tensions between scientists and managers. The scientists will desire consensus; the manager will need to take action, and establish clear numerical standards and targets in the face of scientific uncertainty. Ways of reconciling these approaches include small informal working groups and advisory committees.

Often scientists wish to focus on their own research interests, which may not address the most pressing problems facing managers. Managers should remember that scientists have a need to publish results as a means of career advancement. In order to get scientists to focus on the immediate issues of management, managers may need to offer them incentives.

To sustain a productive relationship between scientists and managers, both parties should try to achieve:

- Common support for the goal and objectives of the programme;

- Mutual understanding of the respective pressures and reward systems under which scientists and managers operate;

- Long-term commitment to progress of the MPA;

- Continuous output of information and progress reports on the monitoring and research programme so as to keep all parties abreast of developments.

9.6   Build capacity for research and monitoring

Managers may need to build local scientific capacity for research and monitoring. This can be done through inter-institutional working groups and mentoring with scientists of international stature, to focus on questions of direct relevance to the MPA and thus help improve the quality and reliability of local work.

It is often better – and usually far less expensive – to bring in existing local scientific institutions as partners, and offer them funding to undertake the work under contract rather than to create a new research institute or department. Where managers do set up a research department, it is vital to make sure it maintains its focus: all too often it ends up pursuing the agenda of research agencies rather than what is needed for effective management.

In developing countries, relying on scientists from developed countries can delay or prevent the establishment of viable MPAs, is usually expensive and may provide results of limited value due to the lack of acculturation. Most serious, it can prevent the development of local capacity. A better approach is to take the time to develop an indigenous cadre of scientists, so that the application of science will continue whether or not foreign scientists are involved. A small team of experienced scientists could be brought in from outside for a short time so as to provide short-term training and help develop the capacity of local scientists.

9.7 Involve the local community in research and monitoring

It is a good idea to involve community groups in the design, conduct and interpretation of research that could lead to management decisions which would seriously affect them. Otherwise they are more likely to deny the validity of the research results and oppose decisions based on those results. A team approach is necessary for real cooperation.

In many cases, local people can undertake much of the information-gathering, as volunteers or for payment. For example fishers could record information on catches and fish stocks, as has happened in the IUCN project to establish a large MPA in Samoa.

9.8 In the planning phase, use research and monitoring to help define the major issues

The most useful input of science in the planning phase is to help define the management issues, why there are problems, and how they should be addressed. The first task of natural scientists is to supply objective data to support or challenge perceptions of resource depletion or degradation. A key role of science is to isolate the causes of the problem and help eradicate misconceptions and prejudices, so that management can then focus on the real causes.

Baselines and monitoring of natural conditions should be in place before the implementation stage, so that an assessment can be made of whether the programme's objectives are being met. It is important to document public perceptions and regulatory procedures from the outset, so that the effectiveness of management can be assessed and appropriate actions taken.

In theory, many technologies, e.g. GIS and remote sensing, are available at the planning phase, but their use is likely to be limited by a lack of time, money and data availability. Premature application of sophisticated technology can divert scarce resources from essential activities.

9.9 In the implementation phase, use research and monitoring to adapt management and as a basis for evaluation

As the MPA programmes mature, the role of science evolves from identifying issues to developing the technologies needed for management and to understanding the results of research, monitoring and feed-back loops. Reporting on success in management is very important; so is reporting on setbacks and failures. The results from monitoring should be used to adapt management, so that management actions have the intended effects.

Typically such work requires a long-term commitment to data collection, management and analysis. Often such long-term data are not available at the time the MPA is created. Often a data set extending over many decades is needed to understand the significance of human impacts as compared to the natural impacts and processes which underpin the functioning of an ecosystem. In the interim, caution should be applied in interpreting results.

As this is a long-term phase, it is important to develop effective long-term working relationships and administrative structures. Ideally, monitoring and research should be supported by long-term funding as part of the core management of the MPA.

In this phase it is worthwhile continuing to use the local community to collect and analyse monitoring information. Local NGOs, for example, can contribute, perhaps to measuring benthic communities at low tide, or assessing coral cover or shellfish stocks. The results of monitoring should be reported back to the community. It is a good idea to include early monitoring of impacts, so that people can quickly see the benefits and gain confidence in the MPA. Many successful conservation programmes have started out with modest aims, but once people have seen the results, it has been possible to expand conservation activities. Visits to other successful sites have also proved useful.

9.10 Reconsider the management programme on the basis of the results of monitoring

This step has been omitted or performed superficially in most MPAs. Yet, if MPAs are to be ecologically and socially sustainable, almost continuous evaluation and learning is essential. Evaluation must address two broad questions:

a) What has been accomplished by the MPA and learned from its successes and failures?

b) How has the context (e.g. environment, governance) changed since the programme was initiated?

The answers to these questions can be used to re-focus management in future.

A meaningful evaluation can be conducted only if the MPA objectives were stated in clear terms and if indicators for assessing progress were identified in the planning phase, and monitored afterwards. Baseline data are essential. Many evaluations yield ambiguous results because these preconditions for assessing performance do not exist.

Natural and social scientists have important roles to play in evaluation. In particular, they should assess the relevance, reliability and cost-effectiveness of scientific information generated by research and monitoring, and advise on the suitability of control data. Such analyses are necessary if funding agencies are to be persuaded that continued investment in scientific work is justified. Scientists should also estimate how far observed changes in managed environments and practices are attributable to MPA measures as opposed to other factors.

9.11 In addition, undertake a formal review at specified intervals

Evaluation should be continuous in any MPA, but it is desirable that there be a commitment to a more formal review some years after the establishment of the MPA and at regular intervals afterwards.

The procedures for a formal review are similar to those used in the planning phase. However, by now there will be established data sets, experienced scientists and managers, and good communications between scientists, managers and community groups, so the exercise should be less demanding. Nevertheless, the formal review can be quite taxing, as it requires participants to identify major problems and failures. Therefore, it is desirable to involve people from outside the established MPA teams, with appropriate skills, knowledge and reputations, who can handle the challenge of self-criticism.

Annexes

Annex 1

Developing a co-management partnership*

There is no "standard recipe" for developing a collaborative management (co-management or CM) partnership, but here are some possible steps for an agency wanting to follow this approach. The concept of co-management is described in Chapter 4.

FIRST STEPS

The typical situation at the beginning could be:

- Many different actors, including governmental representatives at different levels, traditional authorities, interest groups within local communities, NGOs, individuals and private businesses;

- Many points of view on the same marine environment, and many interests and values assigned to it;

- Some form of management that already exists though this is often not discernible to outsiders.

a) Assess the feasibility of a co-management partnership

Before doing anything else, the agency may wish to assess the feasibility of a management partnership. The analysis begins by a realistic evaluation of the existing management system, the system of decision-making (formal and informal), the entitlements to manage and any unrecognized claims. It can also explore the legal and political issues, the institutional context and the economic opportunities, and compare conservation needs with the economic and social needs.

Not all the conditions for feasibility have to be met, but analysing feasibility gives an idea of the obstacles that might have to be met. If the stakeholders are better served without a management agreement, they will have no incentive to enter into the negotiation.

b) Identify the human and financial resources necessary to support the partnership

The process needs "champions" ...it needs energy, passion, willingness, creativity, sacrifice, continuity ... it is not routine work! It also needs knowledge and skills in ecology, social science and economics, and the capacity to communicate with all the stakeholders so as to obtain and keep their confidence.

---

* This chapter is based on material kindly provided by Grazia Borrini-Feyerabend

c)   Create a start-up team.

A start-up team (or initiation committee, launch committee, etc.) is very important at the very beginning. The start-up team is responsible for the initial phase, in which the partnerships are prepared. After that, the stakeholders themselves have to take control of the process.

The start-up team is typically composed of very few people (3 to 5), some from the agency and others from the society at large. All concerned have to be able to identify or communicate with at least one person on the start-up team, even if they do not feel represented by him or her. The key criteria for team members are diversity, credibility and personal motivation. A good team will be active, efficient, multi-disciplinary, transparent in its decision-making, and determined to launch the process but not to lead or dominate it.

PHASE I : PREPARING FOR THE PARTNERSHIP

In the preparatory phase the start-up team:

a)   Gathers information on and makes a preliminary analysis of the main issues at stake and the main problems to be faced

This should cover ecological and socio-economic issues, the management situation (from an historical, cultural, legal, political and institutional perspective), the "actors", and the existing and potential power relations and management conflicts. The results can be summarized in a report, preferably written, to be presented to all the stakeholders at the beginning of the negotiation.

b)   Identifies the units to be managed

On the basis of the above analysis, possible management units can be identified, e.g. a stretch of coastland, a coral reef, a water catchment discharging into the MPA.

c)   Draws up the initial list of potential stakeholders who should participate in management, and develops criteria to differentiate the importance and relative weight of their entitlements ("stakeholder analysis")

The stakeholders include organizations, social groups and individuals with a direct, significant and specific stake in the given territory, area or resources. Potential stakeholders may not yet be clear about their interests and concerns, nor organized to promote them. In most cases, they will have specific management capacities and advantages, will be willing to invest their time and energy, and will be ready to take on specific responsibilities.

d)   Launches and maintains an active process of social communication on the objectives, means and methods of co-management

This can begin by identifying, testing and adopting a name for the co-management process that is culturally valid, inclusive and acceptable (e.g. "our community in the 21st century"). The next step is to ensure a dialogue between the start-up team and the stakeholders, promoting good understanding of the process about to take place and its adoption and transformation into the local context. In this process, the interests and concerns of stakeholders are clarified. It is important too that stakeholders should acknowledge that other interests may be entitled to participate in management.

68

e)   If necessary, helps the stakeholders to organize themselves

To participate in the negotiation, the stakeholders have to arrive at an internal consensus on the values, interests and concerns they wish to bring forward, and have to appoint people to represent them. In some situations the start-up team has to help the stakeholders organize themselves before taking part in the negotiation. Some types of support may be simple (e.g. financing participation at meetings), but others (e.g. supporting the establishment and legal recognition of an organization) may involve more continuous assistance and rather onerous financial commitments. Therefore these can only be evaluated in a specific context.

f)   Identifies and suggests a set of procedures for the negotiation process and, in particular, for the meeting at which the process is launched

This task is one of the team's most important duties. On the basis of the preliminary decisions on the stakeholders and the level of agreement to be reached, the team proposes a schedule of meetings, rules for participation and the level of professional support and facilitation needed. It also obtains agreement on the place, date, working language (or languages), agenda, logistics and necessary facilities at the meeting at which the process is to be launched.

PHASE II: NEGOTIATING AGREEMENTS

Negotiating agreements is at the heart of co-management. It is wise to invest in this process: the management agreements and institutions are only as good as the process that generated them.

The challenge is to develop a partnership through which the benefits and responsibilities of management are shared in the most efficient and equitable manner possible, starting from a situation that may be neither efficient nor equitable.

Before starting it is important to remember that:

- There are many management options, good and bad;

- Given the complexity of ecological and social systems, the best approach is adaptive management ("learning-by-doing");

- Conflicts of interest between the stakeholders are inevitable but can be managed, and all the more so if recognized early on;

- Even when a satisfactory management solution has been found, it will not remain valid for ever; conditions will change and the solutions will have to change in response;

- All the stakeholders (especially the professional experts) should adopt a mature, non-paternalist attitude, and acknowledge the legitimacy of interests and opinions different from their own.

The goal of the negotiation process is a sustainable agreement among the stake-holders on:

- A long-term vision (ecological and social) for the MPA and the surroundings affecting it;

- A short- and medium-term strategy to achieve this vision, with key performance areas, including marine resource management;

- Clear plans, means and institutions to implement the strategy and review it as necessary.

The steps in the negotiation phase are outlined below.

a)   A first meeting on procedures

All stakeholders receive in advance an invitation and a copy of the proposed agenda for the first meeting. The theme may be set quite high e.g. a series of meetings "to understand the main challenges to our marine environment in the next twenty years and prepare together to meet them". An external facilitator is recommended.

Box A1.1 Example of rules for the negotiation process

- All main stakeholders should be present and should participate through their formal representatives;

- Participation is voluntary;

- Language should always be respectful;

- Everyone agrees not to interrupt people who are speaking;

- Everyone agrees on talking only on the basis of personal experience and/or concrete, verifiable facts;

- Everyone agrees not to put the opinions of people who are not attending the meetings;

- Consensus is to be reached on all decisions and voting should be resorted to in exceptional cases only;

- Full confidentiality is to be maintained until agreements are reached;

- Observers are not admitted to the meeting.

The discussion may begin with an introduction by the start-up team, describing its work so far and a proposed schedule of meetings and rules for the negotiation process. It is important to be transparent on who has set up and paid for the team's work, and why.

Procedural aspects, such as who will be present, what language(s) is spoken, what equipment is needed, are generally easier to deal with than questions of substance and relationships among the stakeholders. In the first meeting, therefore, it is good to limit discussion to matters of procedures. An initial meeting in a calm and productive atmosphere is a good way of helping the stakeholders find out where they stand, establish working relations among themselves and start owning the participatory process.

b)   One or more meetings to review the situation and trends, and agree on a long-term, common vision for the MPA and its surroundings

The aim of these meetings is to establish a basis of common interests and concerns among all the institutions involved. To do so, a discussion is facilitated on the present ecological, economic and social situation, and on the desirability and acceptability of current trends.

The discussion can start on the basis of the report submitted by the start-up team, although the report should not define the limits of the discussion. Other good starting points are historical mapping exercises, public interviews with local elders who have experience of the sea, and retreats. Facilitation is highly recommended.

The stakeholders are encouraged to discuss their long-term wishes, i.e. the kind of environment and living conditions they would ideally like to leave to their children. On this basis, the facilitator helps the participants to develop a consensus on a desired vision for the future, with specific descriptions – as visual and concrete as possible – of its ecological, economic and social features.

This consensus is extremely important, as it will need to be transformed into a "charter of principles" or other appropriate form of social contract. In this way, the vision and its features will be regarded as intangible, sacrosanct and non-negotiable, and will apply to society as a whole and not just those taking part in the meetings.

c)   A ceremony to legitimize the agreed common vision

An agreement is legitimized when it is accepted and recognized as binding not only by the stakeholders who developed it, but by society as a whole. This calls for a form of public affirmation, respected and acknowledged by the whole society. This is very specific to the culture, drawing on its moral, spiritual and religious values, and should be confirmed by a ceremony or public event.

To be most effective, the ceremony should include a public declaration of the terms of the agreement – in this case the vision of the agreed, long-term desired future for the MPA and its surroundings. This will help raise the vision to the symbolic level, making it difficult to disavow. The vision will constitute the "basis of common interest and concern" that will help the stakeholders to work together.

When several outside representatives are involved, it is advisable that the stakeholders also produce and sign a written document. In this case, the ceremony could include the celebration and public signing of such a document (e.g. a charter of principles for the marine resource management and development approaches in the relevant surroundings).

d)   One or more meetings to agree on a strategy towards the long-term vision

With the help of a facilitator, the stakeholders analyse the present situation and identify a strategy towards the common, long-term vision. Several techniques can be used, including brainstorming, problem analysis, and the analysis of strengths, weaknesses, opportunities and limitations (SWOL).

At the outset, the present situation is compared with the future vision. What are the problems and obstacles blocking progress? What opportunities, resources and assets can be relied on? After a realistic discussion of these points, attention should focus on identifying the **key performance areas**, i.e. the areas in which it is necessary to act in the short to medium term to achieve the long-term vision ("transform the desirable into the possible"). For each area it is also important to agree on some major desirable objective before discussing specifically what needs to be done to reach that objective.

Some of the key performance areas will deal directly with marine resource management, whereas others may affect it less directly (e.g. through education, health, or social organization). The challenge is not only to identify the key performance areas and related objectives, but to understand and evaluate the links among them.

In this process it is useful to:

■ Identify and analyse problems, their root causes and consequences with respect to the common vision. Can everyone agree on what constitutes a problem affecting the achievement of the vision? Can everyone see the same causes and consequences arising from these problems? It is a good idea to have these problems written on a large sheet of paper and posted on the wall, possibly next to the description of the agreed vision.

■ Break down large issues into smaller or sectoral ones, and assign them to sub-committees or task forces, but maintain times of common discussion and an overall strategic view.

Box A1.2   The role of facilitator or mediator

He/she:

■ Is responsible for the logistics of the meetings;

■ Helps the start-up team and the stakeholders define the rules for the meetings;

■ Ensures that the process takes place in accordance with the agreed rules and that everyone has a fair chance to participate;

■ Makes sure that the representatives of the stakeholders truly represent them and are not merely self-appointed;

■ Promotes the best possible communication among the institutions involved, e.g. by rephrasing points, asking questions, suggesting new ideas to be explored;

■ Helps a group to broaden its range of options;

■ Points out the positive aspects of the process;

■ Does not state his or her opinion and does not decide anything;

■ Lets everyone know when an agreement that has a chance of being sustainable has been found.

A good facilitator is:

■ Recognized as independent;

■ Generally respected by all those involved;

■ Able to relate to everyone;

■ Able to listen;

■ Able to pose the key questions, for example, on the root causes of the various problems and the feasibility of the options put forward;

■ Capable of getting the best out of the participants and helping them see a different future for themselves.

■ Facilitate meetings, a task firmly anchored in the culture of those concerned (see Box A1.2); a task all the more important when there is a strong power imbalance among the parties.

e)   Meetings to define specific agreements (contracts) for each key performance area of the strategy

For each key performance area or component of the strategy, the stakeholders have to identify what needs be done to progress towards the desired future. The objectives identified up to this point are generally broad (e.g. "to extract marine resources around the MPA in a sustainable manner") and have to be translated into work plans that answer specific questions such as who needs to do what, by when, where, how, and with what financial and human resources. This is the moment at which issues become concrete, numerous strategic options and choices are apparent to everyone, different points of view abound, and conflicts surface.

At this time, it is expedient to form working groups for each issue, making sure that those most directly affected are represented in the relevant group. It is also a good idea for each group to have its own facilitator or moderator, perhaps one of the parties who takes on a neutral role learnt by watching the professional facilitator at work (who can remain in the wings for all eventualities).

The groups have to come to terms with the various avenues open to them to achieve the same objective and select the one best suited to the conditions and needs of the given context. The tools already used to arrive at the long-term vision and strategy (e.g. brainstorming, problem analysis, SWOL analysis) can help again, but some other techniques can also be used, notably:

■ **Discussing the hypotheses and basic assumptions** relating to each option, i.e. why it is thought that a certain action will lead to a certain outcome, such as the probability that fish catches will increase if an area is closed to fishing;

■ **Comparing the expected impacts** of various options, whether environmental, social or economic;

■ **Comparing the feasibility** of various options, including questions of cost and timescales;

■ Effective **conflict mediation** on the basis of the long-term, common vision ("coming back to the present from the future").

There are a number of options in the management of an MPA which can be explored with stakeholders to help reach an agreement:

■ The use of **flexible instruments**, such as spatial zoning and time zoning of the MPA and/or detailed conditions for the use of the resources at stake;

■ Asking the stakeholders to devise (and estimate the feasibility) of **incentives** that would encourage them to agree on a given option.

If a small working group does not arrive at a consensus on any of the options, it can present them all to the general meeting and ask the advice of everyone. The assembly may compare the different options according to criteria such as cost or ecological benefit, and may pursue the discussion, perhaps proposing additional compensation or incentives to one option. The aim is to achieve a consensus on the most appropriate course of action for each key component of the strategy.

The course of action agreed for each component then needs to be made binding. This is done by means of formal agreements (e.g. an MPA management plan, a project implementation contract, a municipal by-law) among the group of directly concerned stakeholders and other external bodies as necessary. The management plans for the relevant units of natural resources should specify a share of functions, benefits and responsibilities and be signed by the institutions involved. The more institutions and the more finances involved, the more advisable it is for the agreements to have a legal basis (e.g. as contracts). The signatories should be those individuals who are directly assigned responsibility in the agreement and not the authorities whom they may represent.

All agreements should specify the activities to be undertaken, by whom and how, as well as the anticipated results and impacts to be monitored (generally known as a "follow-up protocol"). They should also specify when those involved will meet again to assess whether the action has been effective and/or needs to be adjusted (evaluation reviews).

Copies of the agreements – written simply and in the local language – should be disseminated to the stakeholders and the public at large. It is important to keep the public informed on everything that happens in the negotiation meetings, and explain why agreements are reached on certain options.

f)   Meetings to set up the institutions needed

Socio-economic development and the management of natural resources require on-going experimentation and learning. Thus, the process of negotiating and implementing agreements is never finished and a relatively stable organization is needed to be in charge of executing and reviewing the agreements. The organizations that may be set up to sustain the agreements may be a formal Board, Council or Trust or an informal association.

g)   Meeting to legitimize the agreements and organizations

The end of the negotiation process is usually marked by a meeting in which the results are made known to the community or public. This meeting is held in the presence of authorities with more extensive powers than those who participated in the negotiations. At the meeting, the stakeholders publicly undertake to respect the agreements, which are presented for all to see. The meeting is also an excellent opportunity to celebrate the work of the stakeholders and the new hope generated by their agreement.

It is important that the agreements and organizations are here reconfirmed and celebrated, but not rendered sacrosanct, as was the vision for the long-term future. On the contrary, agreements and organizations are to be monitored, evaluated and modified continuously, according to their results and performance.

PHASE III: IMPLEMENTING THE AGREEMENTS AND "LEARNING-BY-DOING"

The following occurs in this phase:

a)   The agreements, organizations and rules (including plans for marine resource management) are implemented and enforced

The agreements, organizations and rules should be implemented as soon as possible after their public celebration, to capitalize on the impetus of the negotiation phase.

A committee or specified individual should be in charge of each key performance area, resource management plan or activity, reporting to the stakeholders (and/or the institutions set in place by them) on progress.

Compliance with the agreements and rules is essential to the effectiveness of the whole process. If some disobey the rules, others are soon likely to follow. To prevent this, the agreements need to specify who is responsible for enforcement, what means they have at their disposal and what regular checks they are to carry out.

b)   As necessary, the entitlements and responsibilities of the stakeholders are clarified

In the course of implementing activities, diverging interpretations of the agreements and the rules may surface. For the more formal agreements, contract and environmental law will provide some basic reference. For the less formal agreements, it is important to foresee how conflict will be managed and if possible who could assist as a mediator.

It is also important to avoid the trap of rigid and bureaucratic rules. Co-management feeds on the passion and creativity of the individuals involved, and on their ability to manage human relations in an informal and convivial way.

It often becomes clear during implementation that the effectiveness of the agreed course of action depends on specific changes in a country's policies and laws. As far as possible, these changes should be pursued by the stakeholders.

c)   While agreements are being implemented, data are collected as outlined in the follow-up protocols

In each agreement is a follow-up protocol, which includes the indicators to be monitored and who is to do the monitoring. These indicators are monitored regularly, and the data collected are made accessible to the stakeholders and the general public. Many of these tasks are taken on by local volunteers.

To facilitate learning-by-doing, it is important to collect data but also to adopt an appropriate management attitude. If mistakes are regarded as an opportunity for learning and if people are rewarded for identifying problems and promoting innovative solutions, learning-by-doing will be strongly encouraged.

On the other hand, it is important that innovations, and in particular innovations to management plans agreed by all institutions involved, are not introduced without prior authorization. Even if these innovations are important, they could still invalidate the monitoring, and thus the process of learning-by-doing.

d)   As agreements and plans are pursued, some innovation is experimented with, technical solutions are refined and/or activities are undertaken on a wider scale

Often, unforeseen difficulties and new information arise as soon as the agreements are implemented. These should be documented and as far as possible incorporated in the plans. In due course, however, they should receive the attention of those responsible in the monitoring, evaluation and review meetings.

While the agreements and management plans are being implemented, the people having access to marine resources tend to develop a heightened sense of the legitimacy of their role and responsibility. This may encourage them to refine the management rules and to apply more efficient and complex technical solutions. Moreover, the area covered by the agreements and plans may grow in size, such as when new communities sign the agreement. Implementation may also see the arrival of new individuals or institutions, such as a federation of fishers' associations. This type of innovation – a key element of learning-by-doing – is facilitated by flexible management plans and budgets, and by sensible people in charge.

e)   Review meetings at regular intervals evaluate the results obtained and lessons learnt. If necessary, activities are modified and/or new management plans and agreements developed

Meetings are held at regular intervals to evaluate the results of management agreements and plans. If the activities and commitments are particularly relevant, the evaluation will be both internal (participatory) and external (independent), and the results of those evaluations will be compared and analysed together.

In a participatory evaluation process, the stakeholders examine the environmental and social results and impacts in comparison with those that they expected. They ask themselves whether the management agreements and plans have succeeded in progressing towards the agreed common vision and thus whether the hypotheses on which the work was based were correct. They also ask themselves whether the context has changed, whether lessons have been learned from experience and whether the process is on the right track.

On the basis of these discussions, the stakeholders decide whether the management agreements and plans have to be modified and if so what changes are needed and who should carry them out. The process may revert to a phase of negotiation and mediation, although generally at a faster pace than the first time. It is useful to have an emergency plan for situations in which a fast intervention is needed.

The results of the "learning-by-doing" phase are:

- Agreements and plans for natural resource management implemented and enforced;

- Co-management organizations and rules in operation;

- Continuing clarification and adjustment of the entitlements and responsibilities of the organizations involved;

- Monitoring data collected, analysed and made available (as described in the follow-up protocol);

- Experience with some management innovation;

- Results and impacts of activities, and lessons learnt, evaluated and analysed;

- Activities, management plans and agreements modified on the basis of monitoring and evaluation.

Box A1.3 Tips in developing management partnerships

A few tips for all phases

- Always try to understand the cultural (traditional) roots of the activities to be implemented and rely on them, possibly by fusing traditional and modern management practices;
- Identify and emphasize the benefits derived from the MPA (e.g. regeneration of fish stocks), which may not be sufficiently appreciated but can become effective incentives for sound resource management;
- Recognize and harness the non-economic benefits to individuals in the participatory process (e.g. prestige, social standing, experience, personal contacts);
- Disseminate information on the positive outcomes from co-management and the negotiated agreement (e.g. local authority and responsibility in management; enhanced sustainability of the local environment; promotion of a more mature and responsible society).

Tips for the preparatory phase

- Ensure clarity of purpose in the participatory approach and confidence in the skills of the start-up team: people feel comfortable and perform well only when they understand what is happening;
- Pay great attention to the cultural significance of the language used, including concepts, the name of the process, titles, stories, examples, descriptions of the starting point in the local situation, and description of the common vision, as well as non-verbal messages such as attitudes, clothing, eating and drinking habits, transport;
- Invest in social communication even before launching the process – use all available means to promote discussions on the local environment and living conditions, recruit local artists, broadcast radio interviews, promote special days at schools, invite religious leaders to give special sermons;
- Improve communication among the stakeholders – facilitate informal direct contacts between individuals belonging to different groups and bearing different interests and concerns to the negotiation table, such as sharing transport, eating together or sharing housing facilities;
- Insist that each institution holds an internal discussion on its interests and concerns, and is well organized and prepared to express and uphold them in the negotiation meetings.

Tips for the central phase of negotiation

- The start-up team has to be as transparent as possible (e.g. who are their members and why, what resource allocation they have) and should not be connected to political parties;
- If possible, circulate reports (background papers) before the meetings, but with a note stating that everyone can and should discuss them, correct them and add their contribution;
- Reassure everyone that no solution will be imposed on any of the stakeholders and that the process will take place at a comfortable pace;
- Use professional facilitators, but also train local people in facilitation, so they can act as facilitators in sub-committees, working groups, etc.;
- Evaluate the question of closed or open meetings in the cultural context: beware of observers at negotiation meetings as they can have a powerful negative influence on the process but closed meetings too may cause the excluded to distrust the process;
- Use as many visual aids as possible – maps, videos, photos; make the discussion as concrete as possible; conduct field-trips during negotiations;
- Give all the stakeholders enough time to think and to voice their ideas – problems need to come out and people need to be listened to!

Box A1.3   Tips in developing management partnerships (cont.)

- Use imaginative ways of safeguarding resources (e.g. use based on zoning, leasing, limited permits in certain seasons and only with certain types of fishing gear);
- Appoint sub-committees and working groups to treat specific issues;
- Ask the stakeholders several times whether all main obstacles and problems have been dealt with;
- Probe in depth the feasibility of agreed activities and the availability of means to implement them;
- Involve the authorities personally, by meetings, public events, etc.;
- If one of the stakeholders exerts pressure on the others in the form of corruption or intimidation, the negotiation is no longer valid. The situation may be resolved by higher authorities taking a stand or with an internal dissociation within the group exerting the pressure.

Tips for "learning-by-doing"

- Find someone to be the champion of every major task;
- Promote voluntary activities and offer plenty of social gratification in return;
- Make sure that all those working for the initiative are recognized and appreciated;
- Ensure that any important management change is closely monitored;
- Learn from mistakes, transform them into sources of knowledge, tell stories of what has been learned along the way;
- If community animators are used, make sure that they are chosen by the communities and adequately supported and rewarded;
- Build contacts with colleagues working in other locations and countries, but facing similar problems.

Annex 2

Contents of an MPA Management Plan

This Annex sets out in detail the matters that need to be dealt with in a comprehensive Management Plan for a large MPA. Management Plans for small, relatively simple MPAs can be correspondingly reduced in content. As outlined in Chapter 6, in a large multiple-use MPA, a zoning plan establishes the framework from which the management plan is derived. This means that the zoning plan, rather than the management plan, is the primary document. In a small MPA, the management plan is self-contained and complete. Details of how to prepare a zoning plan are given in Annex 3.

Outline

During the development of plans and associated reports, it is necessary to consider the available information and to determine how far it is appropriate to cover the following items:

- Executive Summary: Covers the essential issues and necessary decisions. Many of the final decision-makers will not have time to read and digest supporting detail;

- Introduction: Defines the purpose and scope of the plan and explains the legislative basis and authority for plan development;

- Statement of the goal and objectives for the planned MPA as a whole;

- Definition of the area: A formal statement on the boundaries of the planned MPA and a geographic description of its setting and accessibility;

- Description of the resources of the area: A summary of information directly relevant to decisions (detail should be restricted to an annex or separate document);

- Description of uses of the area: Concentrates on present uses but should place these in the context of past types and levels of use. This includes social and economic analyses of use;

- Description of the existing legal and management framework, such as coastal fisheries, marine transportation and other relevant legal controls on present use of the area. Where they still exist or can be recalled, traditional practices of management, ownership or rights to the use of marine resources should be described;

- Analysis of constraints and opportunities for activities possible within the area;

- Statement of the principal threats to the conservation, management and maintenance of the area;

- Statement of policies, plans, actions, inter-agency agreements and responsibilities of individual agencies relevant to meet the objectives of the MPA and to deal with threats and conflicts. This may include a summary of consultative processes followed in plan development;

- Statement of the boundaries, objectives and conditions of use and entry for any component zones of the planned area;

- Provision for regulations required to achieve and implement boundaries and conditions of use and entry;

- An assessment of the financial, human and physical resources required to establish and manage the MPA including:

  - staffing

  - equipment and facilities

  - training

  - budget

  - interpretation and education

  - monitoring and research

  - restoration

  - surveillance

  - enforcement

  - contingency/emergency planning

  - evaluation and review of effectiveness.

It is likely that the zoning or management plan will have to be supplemented by separate reports and procedure manuals, which will be developed during the life of the plan. For details regarding zoning plans, see Chapter 7 and Annex 3.

Detailed contents of an MPA management plan

This example of the content of an MPA Management Plan is provided to assist those involved in the preparation of plans and submissions in government agencies and NGOs. It should be viewed as an ideal model, since it implies a planning situation where there is a high level of description and understanding of the area under investigation. The precise format adopted will depend upon the provisions of the legislation establishing the MPA and the government processes required for putting a management plan into effect.

The example that follows is where the management plan is the primary policy-setting document and the zoning plan is subordinate to it. In many cases the items 1– 4.1 may form a preliminary document which establishes the initial case for protection of the area in question.

TITLE PAGE

This includes:

- The name of the area subject to the plan and its status;

- The words MANAGEMENT PLAN;

- The name of the agency/agencies responsible for implementing the plan;

- The date when the plan was prepared and the expected date for review.

EXECUTIVE SUMMARY PAGE

On this page are summarized:

- The reasons why the plan was prepared;

- The period of time to which it applies;

- Any special conditions which controlled its preparation including the legislative basis and authority for plan development;

- The principal provisions of the plan;

- The estimated budget; and

- Acknowledgements.

CONTENTS PAGE

The headings of the body of the plan are listed here against the appropriate page numbers. It may be preferable to list only the main headings, but sub-headings are usually included.

BODY OF THE PLAN

1. Objectives for Management

The goal and objectives for management are stated in this section. They will reflect the purpose(s) for which the area is protected and the use(s) which will be permitted.

2. Resource Description

This section provides information on the following categories for the areas to be protected. Maps will be an important feature of this section.

2.1 Name of Area and Location

To include the geographic location (State, district, etc.); latitudes and longitudes (preferably on a map); surface area (square kilometres, hectares or other units of area).

2.2 Geographic and Habitat Classification

The area should be categorised according to a habitat classification scheme to identify its geographic zone, substrate type(s) and major biological feature(s).

2.3   Conservation Status

This should indicate the area's degree of naturalness, aesthetic values, degree and nature of threats (if any), jurisdiction(s) and present ownership. The degree of habitat representativeness should also be indicated.

2.4   Access and Regional Context

The regional land and sea surroundings and access routes to the area are described, in addition to the character and use of contiguous areas, emphasising their effectiveness as buffer zones.

2.5   History and Development

This section contains a summary account of direct and peripheral human involvement in the area. This section may be divided into several sub-sections e.g.:

2.5.1   Archaeology

A summary description of the people who used the area before historical times, including any known areas of religious significance, species taken and if closed seasons or closed areas were ever used as management techniques. Archaeological information could also provide clues to species that were found in the area.

2.5.2   Historical relics

This sub-section should identify submerged wrecks and any other submerged structures of historic interest.

2.5.3   Written and oral history

2.5.4   Recent developments

Give a brief history of fishing and other human use of the area and developments on the land which may have had a major influence on the area.

2.5.5   Current human use and development

In this section the current use of the area by subsistence, artisanal, commercial and recreational fishermen, tourists and others is discussed. It is most important to establish who the users are, where they conduct their activities, at what times of the year, and for how long, and the social and economic importance of their use. A user survey may be helpful. This information is just as important as biophysical data.

2.6   Physical features

In this section the non-living features of the area are described. Maps in addition to descriptions should be included.

2.6.1   Coastal landforms

Nearby land forms should be described, together with islands and underwater formations.

2.6.2 Bathymetry

A map showing isobaths is needed. The depth of water can provide an important insight into the dynamics of the system. Major trenches, canyons and shallows should be described.

2.6.3 Tides

A description of the tidal regime and resultant currents and water movements associated with phases of the tidal cycle.

2.6.4 Water quality, including salinity, turbidity and other important parameters

Measurements of salinity, turbidity and any major pollutant levels in all seasons are desirable.

2.6.5 Geology

A description in geological terms about how the area was formed and how that process is continuing with the deposition of present day substrates and by erosion processes observable in the area.

2.6.6 Dominant currents

A description of wind-driven, tidal and residual currents, on a seasonal basis.

2.6.7 Freshwater inputs

Major river and estuarine areas.

2.7 Climate

2.7.1 Precipitation

Annual precipitation figures and a chart to indicate average precipitation on a monthly basis.

2.7.2 Temperature

Monthly charts for both air and average sea temperatures (surface and at given depth). If possible include a monthly chart of solar radiation received.

2.7.3 Winds

Monthly charts of rose diagrams plus a description of any unusual feature of the local winds.

2.8 Plant life

This section should contain at least a description of dominant marine plant life, and wherever possible a comprehensive summary of the plant community and related environmental factors, such as the depth of occurrence, together with any botanical features that may have special scientific, recreational or other interest. Phytoplankton could be included if information is available. Plant species identified in the area should be listed in an appendix.

2.9   Marine fauna

As a minimum, a description of the dominant marine or estuarine fauna is required, with an account of their ecological relationships if known. Include sections on Mammals, Reptiles, Amphibians, Fish, Birds, Invertebrates and Zooplankton as appropriate. A separate appendix should list the species.

Note: Sections 2.8 and 2.9 could be amalgamated to one section entitled 'Marine Wildlife'. Wildlife would be defined as: animals and plants that are indigenous to the nation, to its coastal sea, to its continental shelf or its overlying waters; migratory animals that periodically or occasionally visit its territory; and such other animals and plants, not being domesticated animals or cultivated plants, as are prescribed by legislation.

2.10 Miscellaneous

This can be a varied section that includes those matters which do not fit under any of the other descriptions of the plan. Each plan will be site specific and could therefore have features or problems which are not encountered in other plans.

3.   Description of Management Issues

A summary of past, present and possible future threats and management conflicts should follow.

3.1   Historic and current conflicts

A brief statement of any historic or current conflicts between uses or user groups.

3.2   Pollution

Include point and non-point sources of external pollution within the area and in nearby areas, e.g. runoff, sewage inputs, fish processing, industrial pollution and pollution from tourism and shipping.

3.3   Future demand

Estimate future demand for recreational and other uses, and if applicable, future pollution loading and proposed developments.

3.4   Potential conflicts

Potential conflicts specific to the area within and close to the boundary of the MPA should be described. Any potential conflicts due to more distant regional influences should also be identified. This should include review of sectoral development plans and proposed projects which could affect the area.

4.   Management policies

In this section the management plan comes to grips with the threats and conflicts and prescribes solutions.

4.1   Objectives

The goal of protecting the area is briefly reiterated. The objectives of management are stated clearly. If the area is to be subdivided, sub-objectives should be stated for each zone or subdivision of the managed area.

4.2   Resource units

It could be useful to divide the area into resource units.

4.2.1   Natural

Each MPA will have unique characteristics and the resource units will be site specific. An area could be divided into resource units such as beaches, islands, deep water trenches, turtle or seal rookeries etc.

4.2.2   Development areas

Another category could be areas that are either developed or proposed to be developed.

4.2.3   Areas of impact

Areas showing marked impact from human activity could be identified.

4.3   Zoning

The resource units defined above may provide a basis for zoning. Zoning must be easy to understand both from the point of view of the manager and the managed. This section should explain why a particular area has been given a zone classification and what activities are permitted and prohibited within each zone. The aim should be to keep the zoning arrangements as simple as possible, consistent with avoiding unnecessary restriction on human activities.

Special habitats or wildlife areas such as a seagrass bed or a turtle rookery, may require additional management provisions, such as seasonal closures or permanent restrictions over access. Unusual prescriptions may be needed in the short term and these should be described in this section.

4.4   Management policies for resource units

In the draft management plan a list of management options can be presented and a choice made between them in the final version of the plan.

5.   Surveillance

This section should describe any programmes proposed to assess movement of people, vessels and aircraft within and through the area and the use made of the area.

6.   Monitoring

This section should describe any biological, environmental and usage monitoring programmes proposed for the area, when these programmes will be completed and how they are to be used in reviewing the management plan. It may also identify other monitoring programmes to be initiated during the first stage of the plan and who could carry them out. Some of the results from monitoring may eventually be included in the appendices.

7.   Education and Interpretation

This section should describe programmes and co-operative arrangements with educational institutions, public associations and community groups to promote protection, wise use, public understanding and enjoyment of the MPA. Co-management may be an option.

8. Enforcement

This section should outline the arrangements which will need to be made to detect apparent offences and to apprehend and prosecute offenders in order to achieve an acceptable level of adherence to MPA regulations. **It is absolutely unrealistic to manage primarily on the basis of enforcement in the face of general public hostility** or to apprehend every breach of regulation. Education, community involvement and "ownership" are therefore the primary management tools.

9. Maintenance and Administration

A section will be required to address the subjects of budget, staffing, etc.

9.1 Budget

Anticipated costs and possible sources of funds should be identified with the aim of achieving a high level of self-financing.

9.2 Staffing

The management plan should indicate staffing needs and identify major functions. Volunteers, consultants and head office staff involved in the planning process should also be identified, as this will provide a more accurate indication of staffing levels. Staffing deficiencies can be predicted and recommendations suggested. Section 9 should be updated and released as part of an annual report.

10. Information Sources

Information regarding the area will come from sources outside the manager's regular information base. These should be identified and listed wherever possible, and include those other government agencies, non-government organisations, individuals, consultants, overseas sources etc. that were consulted.

A bibliography should be appended.

11. Appendices

Appendix 1: Boundary and Area Description

This should provide the legal description of the area including any outstanding legal tenure or matters of existing interest which might have become clear during the development of the management plan. In most federal systems of government, there are complex and sometimes unresolved questions of jurisdiction between levels of government especially in the intertidal environment. These problems should be highlighted and, if appropriate, solutions suggested. One solution is to have complementary legislative, planning and management provisions on each side of that jurisdictional boundary. Examples of this include adjacent Federal and State Marine Protected Areas at Florida Keys and the Californian Channel Islands in the USA and the Great Barrier Reef Marine Park and adjacent Queensland Marine Parks in Australia.

Appendix 2: Legislation

All legislation and regulations relating to the area, and their interactions, should be noted and explained. Where feasible, the legislation that prevails in the event of conflict between the provisions of different enactments should be identified. Implications for the protective status of the area should be identified.

Appendix 3: Plant Species

A comprehensive list of plant species should be attempted for the first management plan. As the process continues over the years, it is quite possible that new plant species will be discovered in the area. Plant names should be listed in broad taxonomic groups, with botanical and common names where possible.

Appendix 4: Animal Species

Animal species should be listed in broad taxonomic groups: e.g. Mammals, Reptiles, Amphibians, Fish, Birds and Invertebrates and common names provided where possible.

Appendix 5: Special Features

This section could describe unusual or outstanding features of the area and could range from whale strandings, waterspouts, oil slicks to spiritual revelations and cultural beliefs.

Appendix 6: Past, Present and Proposed use

This section should attempt to provide more detail on uses, identify key user groups and assess the social and economic significance of areas.

Maps

The following are suggested as a minimum number of maps required:

Map 1	Location
Map 2	Land/water tenure and jurisdiction
Map 3	Land topography and seabed bathymetry
Map 4	Geology
Map 5/6	Dominant plant and animal communities
Map 7/8	Major uses
Map 9	Major use conflicts and threatened resources
Map 10	Zoning

Where practicable the use of overlay presentation is recommended in order to illustrate the associations between such factors as topography, biological communities and uses.

Annex 3

Detailed guidelines on how to make a Zoning Plan[*]

1. Initial Information Gathering and Preparation

The initial task of the planning team is to assemble and review available information on the resources and use of the area to be planned and, if the area is already under management, on the experience, effectiveness and performance of management. From this initial review specific investigations may be identified as necessary to provide important information within the available time frame for the current planning operation. A review document is then developed by the planning team.

The review document provides the basis for public participation materials. The form of these materials will depend upon the scale of the area and the most appropriate means of communicating with the community concerned.

For a large-scale planning operation in a community with a high level of literacy, the information might be distributed most widely through a **brochure** which describes the purpose of the programme and the process of plan development, and which invites interested readers to contact the planning agency for further information. The brochure should incorporate a map, a questionnaire and a paid, mail-back panel in order to make it as easy as possible for a respondent to make a representation.

A more substantial **published document** might also be used. It should be a jargon-free summary of about 50 pages, provided to interested individuals and groups or sent to those who request further information after reading the brochure. This document should seek to draw out the issues which must be faced in developing the plan. A major part should be maps illustrating the distribution of resources and usage patterns.

Typical Resource and Activity Maps

These may be produced manually as transparent overlays or by computer using Geographic Information System (GIS) software – see Box A3.1.

Preparations for public participation require the development of a theme for the brochure, and an advertising programme for the media (press, television and radio where appropriate) which will attract public attention.

A user-friendly, culturally appropriate approach is recommended, with the aim of encouraging public involvement. An approach based on cartoons has proved successful in some cases.

The final element of preparation involves arrangements to publicize and distribute the brochure and other materials. Summaries and brochures should be mailed to a large

---

[*]Much of the material in this Annex is drawn from Kenchington, R, (1990) *Managing Marine Environments*.

Box A3.1   Typical resource and activity maps needed

1   Distribution of fish and benthic communities

2   Endangered, rare or protected species distribution and significant sites (eg. Dugong, turtle, manatee, whales, seals)

3   Significant colonies of breeding birds

4   Mangrove, sea-grass and kelp forest communities

5   Trawling

6   Pelagic fishery (e.g. mackerel, cod)

7   Demersal fishery (commercial, recreational)

8   Netting (gill and drift, bait)

9   Collecting (coral, shells, aquarium fish)

10   Spearfishing

11   Diving

12   Sites used for research and scientific study

13   Tourist developments including camping

14   Charter vessels and aircraft

15   Adjacent land use (eg. National Park, trust land, industrial use, agriculture)

16   Navigation, shipping and defence areas

17   Mariculture/fish farming

18   Traditional uses and rights

---

number of groups and individuals. Other means of distribution may be through small promotional display panels. These can be set up on shop counters and in offices of organizations which have an interest in the area affected. A schedule of meetings will be needed to accommodate requests by interested groups to discuss the plans with staff of the planning agency.

In countries where the social tradition is face-to-face contact with the community, with little or no history of distribution of information in written or electronic form, the approach should, of course, be adapted through the use of socially appropriate techniques to convey explanatory information. These might include village drama, story-telling, tee-shirts or church meetings.

2.   Public Participation or Consultation - Prior to Preparing a Plan

The primary function of this phase is to inform users and others interested in the MPA, directly or through their representatives, that a zoning plan is to be prepared. It is used to seek comment and correction of maps and other information on resources and their use. It should also solicit opinions on the provisions to be included in the zoning plan. It is important to make direct contact with major stakeholders – relying on advertisements or displays is not enough. Where the planning programme involves the review of an existing zoning plan, this phase can be used as an opportunity to test user reaction to the existing arrangements.

In the absence of specific zoning proposals, most respondents may have generally supportive views on the need for management but little, if any, detailed information to add and few specific proposals. Thus it is important to stress the information function of this phase of the programme. Respondents will be able to comment on specific proposals in the subsequent public participation programme.

3.   Preparation of Draft Plan

The aim is to make a zoning plan as simple as practicable, consistent with providing the necessary protection and **avoiding unnecessary restrictions on human activity**. Specific objectives are defined for each proposed zone. For instance, the most highly protected zone might have the following objective:

> "To provide for the preservation of the area in its natural state, undisturbed by human activities."

By contrast, the least restrictive zone might have the following objective:

> "To provide opportunities for reasonable general use, consistent with the conservation of the Marine Protected Area."

Between these two extremes there will be other zones with intermediate levels of protection.

The planning team should work to guidelines, each expressed with the preamble "as far as practicable" and setting out an objective, e.g. "as far as practicable, a zone for recreational fishing should be provided near a coastal town". Taken together, these guidelines should include all the uses and objectives to be provided for in the zoning plan. They may often be in mutual conflict. Resolution of these conflicts is best achieved through careful consideration of the political, social and ecological factors involved. The guidelines used in the development of zoning plans for the Great Barrier Reef Marine Park are listed as an example in Box A3.2.

Despite the unavoidable conflict between some of the guidelines, in general most zone allocation decisions will follow logically from the guidelines. There are a few "toss-up" allocations where one of several, apparently similar areas could logically be allocated to a restrictive zone. There are some sites, usually those near islands or most accessible from harbours or boat launching ramps where there are clear conflicts of use, and the resolution of which will please one party but displease another. The planning team should develop a draft plan and, if necessary, alternative options for specific problem sites. These should be considered carefully by the planning agency which adopts a plan for release for the second phase of public participation.

The agency should publish a report containing information, updated as necessary since the initial public participation programme, explaining the basis for zoning and presenting a brief summary of specific reasons for restrictive zoning of any areas. These documents are used to develop second phase public participation materials which follow the style and promotional design theme adopted for the initial phase. These might be a 50 page summary and a brochure containing a zoning map, a summary of zoning provisions, a list of questions concerning information of interest to the planning agency and a mail back panel for easy response.

### 4.	Public Participation or Consultation, Review of Draft Zoning Plan

This stage can be conducted similarly to the initial phase. The summary and brochure can be widely distributed by mail using a mailing list expanded to include all those who responded to the initial public participation plan. Counter-top displays can be used again and meetings should be arranged with major stakeholders and in response to user requests. This phase is usually easier to conduct, since users find it much easier to evaluate and react to specific proposals. Material and presentations emphasize that the proposal is not final but is a **draft** to invite public comment. Respondents who wish to object are invited to specify their objections, to propose alternative solutions and to support their arguments with factual evidence where possible. Those who support all or specific parts of the plan are asked to say so in representations. In the absence of that information, a revision to modify a plan to meet an objection by one user group may unwittingly overturn a solution regarded as good by another.

Public comments and suggestions should be summarized as they are received. Usually there will be considerable repetition in these comments. Progress reports on the analysis should be produced as required during the programme. The aim is to produce a detailed analysis within a few weeks of the closure of public consultation.

### 5.	Plan Finalization

The planning team should meet after the report on the analysis of public comments has been completed to consider the issues raised in the public participation exercise and to discuss and evaluate possible changes to the published draft plan.

Proposed major changes should be discussed with those user groups who will be affected by those changes. **The importance of doing this cannot be over-emphasized**. It is often necessary to go through several cycles of consultation so that all changes arising during consultation are discussed with those affected.

The content of the final plan should be determined by the planning agency. After the completion of precise cartographic and written boundary definitions for all zones and checks by the agency's legal officers, the plan should be submitted to the responsible Minister or senior decision-maker for approval.

### 6.	Management and Analysis of Public Participation

Clearly, the appropriate form of public participation or consultation will depend greatly on the social and political context. The description which follows contains a number of principles which may be adapted to a variety of consultative processes. General principles of participation are given in Chapters 3 and 4.

Considerable effort should be put into the management of the public participation exercise to make them efficient and non-bureaucratic. In some communities there may be apathy and cynicism expressed in such terms as "Why bother? You're only asking because the law says you have to. Nothing that I say will make any difference - in any case you probably won't even read it."

The first focus of effort should be to make public participation materials attractive and clearly expressed. The second should be to ensure that trained staff can always be contacted at times convenient to users in order to ensure that:

■	Questions are answered immediately or, with explanation to the caller, referred to a named expert officer;

■	Requests for the materials are responded to promptly; and

■ Requests for meetings with planning staff are logged and arrangements made for them to be fulfilled.

Feedback to the public is important in obtaining support. When a written comment is received, it should be recorded and an acknowledgement sent as soon as possible. The names and addresses of the respondents should be entered in a mailing list so that they can subsequently receive a letter and a copy of the materials developed as a result of the public participation exercise. After the first phase, respondents should receive a letter thanking them again for their participation and a copy of the 50 page information summary and brochure for the second phase. At the conclusion of the process, all participants should receive a copy of the plan and second phase participants should receive a letter which briefly presents the planning agency's response to the issues they raised.

The form and style of written comments will vary. More people will no doubt use the mail-back brochure and respond to the questions upon it. A few may choose to provide detailed technical analyses and arguments covering many pages.

Reports should refer to individual written comments by index number so that it is possible for a planning team member to retrieve all comments about a particular location or activity.

Reports should be produced which cite the number and the points of origin of written comments received. These provide an important indication of the geographic extent of effective contact and involvement of the public participation process.

While the structure and the promotion of the public participation programmes should be designed specifically to obtain comment from interested parties, the results should be treated cautiously, since the programmes will not establish statistically representative samples of the opinion of the public generally or of subsets of the public.

Participants and agency personnel should not regard public comments as "votes". Each expression of interest should be carefully evaluated whether it is made by one person or hundreds of people.

Even so, the responses will allow the agency to assess the breadth of opinion, and permit some cautious expression of public support for, or opposition to, a particular proposition.

The system should be designed to ensure that each written comment is taken into account and that the competing views of the various interest groups can be seen in context.

7. Zoning Plans as a Multiple Management Approach

Zoning plans may use a combination of area-based and other forms of controls. The provisions of the zoning plan should establish purposes and conditions relating to the use of the zones, for example:

■ A use or purpose of entry may be "**of right**" – that is any person may undertake that use or enter the area, subject to any condition specified in the plan;

■ A use or purpose of entry may be allowed only after **prior notification** of the management agency;

■ A use or purpose of entry may be allowed only with a **permit**; or

■ A use or purpose of entry not covered by one of the above may be allowed under the general category of a use "consistent with the objectives of the zone". (Such a general category is needed to avoid the unintended prohibition of uses that were not thought of when the zoning plan was made.)

Box A3.2 Example of guidelines used to make zoning decisions: The Great Barrier Reef Marine Park

These guidelines were used in the preparation of zoning plans for several sections of the Great Barrier Reef Marine Park. Each section covers a large area, of the order of $70,000km^2$. Each section of the Park is in effect a large MPA.

Each section incorporates highly protected (IUCN categories I or II) zones. Other zones provide for a range of multiple uses such as commercial and recreational fishing, mariculture and tourism.

The guidelines used in the Great Barrier Reef Marine Park may be adapted for use wherever zoning of MPAs of any size is appropriate. However, in zoning a small MPA which is surrounded by areas managed for sustainable use, there may be no need to provide for commercial and recreational activities within the MPA.

General, Legislative and Management Requirements

1. The zoning plan should be as simple as practicable.

2. The plan should minimize the regulation of, and interference in, human activities, consistent with meeting the goal of providing for protection, restoration, wise use, understanding and enjoyment of the MPA in perpetuity.

3. As far as practicable, the plan should be consistent with existing zoning plans in the country's other MPAs.

4. As far as practicable, the pattern of zones within the MPA should avoid abrupt transitions from highly protected areas to areas of relatively little protection. The concept of buffering should be applied so that highly protected zones are generally adjacent to, or surrounded by, zones which provide for moderate protection.

5. As far as practicable, single zonings should surround areas with a discrete geographic description, e.g. an island or reef.

6. As far as practicable, zoning boundaries should be described by geographical features (based on line of sight to aid identification in the field).

7. As far as practicable, zoning plans should complement current regulations and management practices.

Conservation of Significant Habitat

1. As far as practicable, areas of world, regional or local significance to threatened species (for example, dugong, seals, whales, turtles, crocodiles) should be given appropriate protective zoning.

Box A3.2   Example of guidelines used to make zoning decisions: The Great Barrier Reef Marine Park (cont.)

2.   As far as practicable, significant spawning, breeding or nursery sites should be given a high degree of protection, particularly for species subjected to harvesting (e.g. with IUCN Category I or II zoning, or by appropriate Seasonal Closure or Replenishment Area designation).

3.   As far as practicable, sources of coral and other sedentary species' larvae which replenish other areas should be identified in "source-sink" studies of larval movement and settlement, and given highly protected status by zoning.

4.   As far as practicable, representative samples of characteristic habitat types should be included in IUCN Category I or II zones.

5.   As far as practicable, protective zoning should be applied to a wide range of habitat types within one unit (e.g. reef/shoal complexes).

National Parks, Reserves and Historic Shipwrecks

As far as practicable, zoning of reefs and waters adjacent to existing National Parks, fisheries reserves and historic shipwrecks should complement the objectives of those reserves.

Commercial and Recreational Activities

1.   As a general rule, areas recognized and/or used for reasonable extractive activities (uses that involve removing any animal, plant or object) should be zoned for general use.

2.   As a general rule, areas of significance for non-extractive activities should be given IUCN Category I or II zoning.

3.   When a reef or reefs are zoned to exclude a particular activity, provision should be made for access to alternative areas as far as possible.

Traditional Hunting and Fishing

Where there is a continuing tradition of hunting or fishing by local inhabitants using appropriate methods for subsistence or cultural reasons, this should be normally allowed in the plan. However, where target species are endangered or very scarce, it may be necessary to restrict or exclude such traditional use. Nevertheless, as far as practicable, provision should be made for traditional hunting and fishing by indigenous people in protected areas.

Anchorages

Zoning of major anchorage sites should permit most current overnight or longer anchoring of vessels to continue. The plan should retain access for small boats to important all-weather anchorages. Access to all zones during emergency conditions should always be allowed. Ideally, in sensitive and potentially heavily used areas, the need for anchoring should be removed by the provision of moorings and a requirement that these should be used.

Box A3.2   Example of guidelines used to make zoning decisions: The Great Barrier Reef Marine Park (cont.)

Shipping

The plan must not impede the access of commercial shipping along recognized, or proposed, shipping routes or to existing ports on the coast. Nor should it impede access to potential ports.

Defence Areas

The plan must recognize defence requirements.

Scientific Research

Provision should be made for the conduct of scientific research throughout the MPA. However, areas should be zoned exclusively for scientific research only where existing and probable future research programmes indicate that they are likely to be used for that purpose on a frequent and regular basis.

Annex 4

Resolutions 17.38 and 19.46 of the IUCN General Assembly

17.38 Protection of the coastal and marine environment

AWARE that the area of sea and seabed is more than two-and-a-half times as great as the total area of land masses of the world, that less than 1% of that marine area is currently within established protected areas and that protection of the marine environment lags far behind that of the terrestrial environment;

RECOGNIZING that the immense diversity of marine and estuarine animals, plants, and communities is a vital component of self-sustaining systems of local, regional, national and international significance and is an integral part of the natural and cultural heritage of the world;

CONCERNED that there are already areas which have become seriously degraded by the direct or indirect effects of human activities and that the rate of degradation is increasing rapidly;

RECOGNIZING that consideration must be given for the continued welfare of people who have customarily used marine areas;

BELIEVING that there are national and international responsibilities for the proper stewardship of the living and non-living resources of coastal and deeper ocean seas and the seabed to ensure their maintenance and appropriate use for the direct benefit and enjoyment of present and future generations;

BELIEVING that the development of such stewardship will require co-ordination and integrated management of a number of potentially competing uses at international, regional, national and local levels;

RECOGNIZING that a number of initiatives have been taken at international, regional and national levels for the establishment of marine protected areas and for managing the use of marine areas on a sustainable basis, including:

- the Regional Seas Programme of the United Nations Environment Programme (UNEP);
- the Man and the Biosphere Programme of the United Nations Educational, Scientific and Cultural Organization (UNESCO);
- the Marine Science Programme of UNESCO;
- the South Pacific Regional Environment Programme;
- initiatives of the Food and Agriculture Organization of the United Nations (FAO), the International Maritime Organization (IMO), the International Whaling Commission (IWC) and other international organizations;

– the proclamation of marine protected areas by 69 nations;

The General Assembly of IUCN, at its 17th Session in San Jose, Costa Rica, 1-10 February 1988:

1. **CALLS** upon national governments, international agencies and the non-governmental community to:

    a) Implement integrated management strategies to achieve the objectives of the World Conservation Strategy in the coastal and marine environment and in so doing to consider local resource needs as well as national and international conservation and development responsibilities in the protection of the marine environment;

    b) Involve local people, non-governmental organizations, related industries and other interested parties in the development of these strategies and in the implementation of various marine conservation programmes.

2. **DECIDES ITSELF** and further **RECOMMENDS** to FAO, IMO, IWC, the legal instrument bodies of the North Sea, UNEP, UNESCO, other international organizations and all nations, that:

    a) The following primary goal be adopted: "To provide for the protection, restoration, wise use, understanding and enjoyment of the marine heritage of the world in perpetuity through the creation of a global, representative system of marine protected areas and through the management in accordance with the principles of the World Conservation Strategy of human activities that use or affect the marine environment";

    b) As an integral component of marine conservation and management, each national government should seek cooperative action between the public and all levels of government for development of a national system of marine protected areas. The term "marine protected areas" is defined as: "Any area of intertidal or subtidal terrain, together with its overlying waters and associated flora, fauna, historical and cultural features, which has been reserved by legislation to protect part or all of the enclosed environment";

    c) Such a system should have the following objectives:

        – to protect and manage substantial examples of marine and estuarine systems to ensure their long-term viability and to maintain genetic diversity;

        – to protect depleted, threatened, rare or endangered species and populations and, in particular to preserve habitats considered critical for the survival of such species;

        – to protect and manage areas of significance to the lifecycles of economically important species;

        – to prevent outside activities from detrimentally affecting the marine protected areas;

        – to provide for the continued welfare of people affected by the creation of marine protected areas; to preserve, protect, and manage historical and cultural sites and natural aesthetic values of marine and estuarine areas, for present and future generations;

— to facilitate the interpretation of marine and estuarine systems for the purposes of conservation, education, and tourism;

— to accommodate within appropriate management regimes a broad spectrum of human activities compatible with the primary goal in marine and estuarine settings;

— to provide for research and training, and for monitoring the environmental effects of human activities, including the direct and indirect effects of development and adjacent land-use practices.

d) The development by a nation of such a system will be aided by agreement on a marine and estuarine classification system, including identified biogeographic areas; and by review of existing protected areas, to establish the level of representation of classification categories within those areas, which may require:

— determination of existing and planned levels of use of the marine and estuarine environment and the likely effects of those uses;

— delineation of potential areas consistent with the objectives listed above and determination of priorities for their establishment and management;

— development and implementation of extensive community education programmes aimed at specific groups, to stimulate the necessary community support and awareness and to achieve substantial self-regulation;

— allocation of sufficient resources for the development and implementation of management plans, for regulatory statutory review processes, interpretation, education, training, volunteer programmes, research, monitoring, surveillance and enforcement programmes.

19.46 Marine and Coastal Area Conservation

APPRECIATING that the marine realm comprises approximately 70 per cent of the Earth's surface and harbours a major share of the planet's biological wealth;

AWARE that the coastal zone is the home of an increasing majority of the world's human population and that the well-being of coastal waters including the maintenance of marine biological diversity is critical to achieving globally sustainable development;

CONCERNED that the world's oceans are subject to increasing human use and misuse which is resulting in the loss of marine biological diversity, and that growing development in coastal areas is the cause of severe impacts on the marine environment;

FURTHER CONCERNED that efforts devoted to marine conservation, including the establishment and management of marine protected areas, lag far behind those for the terrestrial environment and that present levels of resources and programmes are insufficient to address the urgency and complexity of the tasks at hand;

RECOGNIZING that the need for integrated management of coastal and marine environments has been identified as a global priority in many fora and documents including:

— the World Conservation Strategy (1980);

— *Caring for the Earth* (1991);

— Chapter 17 of Agenda 21 (UNCED, 1992);

— *Parks for Life - the Proceedings of the IV World Congress on National Parks and Protected Areas* (1992); and

— *Global Marine Biological Diversity: A Strategy for Building Conservation into Decision Making* (1993);

RECOGNIZING that the UN Convention on the Law of the Sea (UNCLOS) will come into effect in 1994 and may provide appropriate mechanisms for the management of marine resources, including protected areas, beyond the limits of national jurisdiction;

FURTHER RECOGNIZING that to achieve these aims will require the development of considerable management capacity by nations and institutions; substantial changes in practices for management of catchments and coastal lands; development of conservation tools for coastal areas to safeguard sensitive and fragile habitats; and that marine protected areas will need to operate within these developing management systems;

AWARE of the support of governments and the international community for programmes which promote marine conservation involving marine protected areas and other initiatives, including:

— the Regional Seas Programme of the United Nations Environment Programme (UNEP);

— the Man and Biosphere Programme of the United Nations Educational, Scientific and Cultural Organization (UNESCO);

— the Intergovernmental Oceanographic Commission of UNESCO;

— the Marine Science Programme of UNESCO;

— the South Pacific Regional Environment Programme;

— initiatives of the Food and Agriculture Organization of the United Nations (FAO), the International Maritime Organization (IMO), the International Whaling Commission (IWC), The World Bank, the United Nations Development Programme (UNDP) and other international organizations;

ALSO AWARE that IUCN's Commission on National Parks and Protected Areas (CNPPA) is promoting the establishment of a global representative system of marine protected areas to implement Resolution 17.38 of the 17th Session of the General Assembly;

NOTING that, in accordance with the revised System of Classification of Terrestrial and Marine Protected Areas adopted by CNPPA following the IVth

World Congress on National Parks and Protected Areas in 1992, all marine areas of the world are eligible for consideration for protected area status and that in a global representative system some of these areas should be established with a wilderness classification;

NOTING the support of the Vth World Wilderness Congress, meeting in Tromsö, Norway, in September 1993, for coastal nations to establish representative systems of marine protected areas, including areas with wilderness designation, and the recommendation that appropriate international agencies establish protected areas in international marine waters including areas designated as wilderness;

ACKNOWLEDGING the publication of *Global Marine Biological Diversity: A Strategy for Building Conservation into Decision Making*, as a contribution to the Global Biodiversity Strategy, by IUCN, the United Nations Environment Programme, The World Bank, the World Wildlife Fund - US and the Center for Marine Conservation;

NOTING that *Global Marine Biological Diversity* compiles recommendations for marine conservation from Agenda 21, *Caring for the Earth*, the IVth World Congress on National Parks and Protected Areas and other fora and sources;

The General Assembly of IUCN – The World Conservation Union, at its 19th Session in Buenos Aires, Argentina, 17–26 January 1994:

1. **CALLS UPON** governments, international agencies and the non-governmental community:

   a) to give priority to the establishment and support of conservation programmes to achieve integrated management of coastal lands and waters, shallow sea and marine environments, addressing the long-term sustainable requirements of nations, regions and the global community;

   b) to involve all levels and relevant agencies of government, local communities, non-governmental organizations, related industries and other interested parties in the development of strategies and the implementation of programmes;

   c) to encourage coastal nations, where indigenous and traditional use of the sea is to be affected, to include indigenous and local people as partners in the discussions and in any substantial steps involving planning, development, management and maintenance of these areas;

   d) to provide resources to build and support in each coastal nation, and in regional communities of nations sharing common waters, the capacity to develop and implement integrated sustainable management of coastal, shallow sea and marine environments and resources;

   e) to provide incentives and resources to develop effective global networks of peer support to enhance management capacity and training to maximize the sharing between nations and regions of the global community of experience, research and technical information on integrated management of coastal, shallow sea and marine environments and resources to achieve sustainable development;

f) to define and designate responsibilities and mechanisms for marine conservation and for resolving resource use conflicts;

g) to encourage coastal nations to establish under national legislation representative systems of marine protected areas, including areas with wilderness designation;

h) to encourage, under appropriate international mechanisms, the establishment of protected areas, including areas designated as wilderness, in areas beyond the limits of national jurisdiction;

2. **REQUESTS** the Director General as soon as practicable and within available resources:

a) to implement the recommendations of the review of the IUCN Marine and Coastal Areas Programme including promotion of marine protected areas beyond the scope of national jurisdictions;

b) to bring to the attention of all governments, the urgent need for rapid development and application of policies and tools specifically for the conservation of their marine areas;

c) to implement a programme of global evaluation of policies and tools specifically for the conservation of the coastal areas of the world;

d) to convene a high profile workshop on the theme of marine and coastal conservation, which covers all marine aspects of IUCN's programmes, at the next General Assembly of IUCN;

3. **DECIDES** itself to reiterate and recommends to FAO, IMO, The World Bank, the Global Environment Facility, UNEP, UNDP, UNCLOS and other concerned organizations, the primary goal of IUCN General Assembly Recommendation 17.38:

"To provide for the protection, restoration, wise use, understanding and enjoyment of the marine heritage of the world in perpetuity through the creation of a global, representative system of marine protected areas and through the management in accordance with the principles of the World Conservation Strategy of human activities that use or affect the marine environment";

4. **DECIDES** itself and further recommends to the above organizations that the following goal be adopted in respect to integration of the management of coastal, shallow sea and marine resources:

"To contribute to the achievement of sustainable development of coastal and marine areas and resources through the establishment and operation of effective mechanisms to manage in an integrated and anticipatory way all human activities which have impacts on coastal and marine environments and associated people";

5. **RECOMMENDS** that IUCN join the co-sponsors of *Global Marine Biological Diversity*, in establishing and participating in the International Marine Conservation Network as a means of promoting attention and co-operation among government, non-governmental and private organizations for marine conservation.

Annex 5

References

Agardy, T. (1997). *Marine Protected Areas and Ocean Conservation*. Academic Press/Environmental Intelligence Unit, R.G. Landes Co., Texas, USA.

Australian Committee for IUCN (1986). *Australia's Marine and Estuarine Areas – A Policy for Protection*. Occasional Paper No. 1

Council of Nature Conservation Ministers (1995). *Summary Report of the Second Technical Workshop on Selection and Management of Marine and Estuarine Protected Areas, February 15-21 1985. Jervis Bay*. Australian National Parks and Wildlife Service, Canberra, Australia.

Davey, A.G. (1998). *National System Planning for Protected Areas*. IUCN, Gland, Switzerland and Cambridge, UK.

Dobbin, James A. (1976). *Planning, Design, and Management of Marine Parks and Reserves*. Harvard University.

Great Barrier Reef Marine Park Authority (1985). *Zoning the Central Section*. Townsville, Australia.

GESAMP (1996). *The contributions of science to integrated coastal management*. GESAMP Reports and Studies No. 61. FAO, Rome, Italy.

Gubbay, S. (Ed.) (1995). *Marine Protected Areas: Principles and Techniques for Management*. Chapman and Hall, London.

Gubbay, S. (1996). *Marine Refuges: The Next Steps for Nature Conservation and Fisheries Management in the North-east Atlantic?* Report to WWF-UK, Godalming, UK.

Hall, S.J. (1998). Closed areas for fisheries management – the case consolidates. *Trends in Ecology and Evolution* **13(8)**: 297–298.

Harmon, D. (Ed) (1994). *Coordinating research and management in protected areas*. IUCN, Cambridge, UK and Gland, Switzerland.

Hooten, A.J. and Hatziolos, M.E. (1995). *Sustainable Financing Mechanisms for Coral Reef Conservation: Proceedings of a Workshop*. Environmentally Sustainable Development Proceedings, Series No. 9, World Bank, Washington, DC.

Hough, John L. (1998). *Financing marine protected areas: the role of the GEF. PARKS* **8(2)**: 55–59.

IUCN (1976). *An International Conference on Marine Parks and Reserves: papers and proceedings of an international conference held in Tokyo, Japan, 12–14 May, 1975*. IUCN, Morges, Switzerland.

IUCN (1980). *World Conservation Strategy – Living Resource Conservation for Sustainable Development*. IUCN, Gland, Switzerland.

IUCN (1994). *Guidelines for Protected Area Management Categories*. IUCN, Cambridge, UK and Gland, Switzerland.

IUCN (1998). 1997 *United Nations List of Protected Areas*. IUCN, Cambridge, UK and Gland, Switzerland.

Ivanovici, A. (Ed.) (1984). *Inventory of Declared Marine and Estuarine Protected Areas in Australian Waters*. Spec. Publ. 12, Australian National Parks and Wildlife Service, Canberra, Australia.

Ivanovici, A. (1986). Marine and Estuarine Protected Areas (MEPAs) – A national perspective. *Proc. Nat. Conf. on Coastal Management* **(3)**: 149–156. New South Wales State Pollution Control Commission, Sydney, Australia.

Kelleher, G., Bleakley, C. and Wells, S. (1995). *A Global Representative System of Marine Protected Areas*. Great Barrier Reef Marine Park Authority, The World Bank, and IUCN, Washington, D.C. 4 vols.

Kelleher, G. and Lausche B. (1988). Review of Legislation. In *Coral Reef Management Handbook*. UNESCO, Jakarta. Indonesia.

Kelleher, G. and Recchia, C. (Eds) (1998). Marine Protected Areas. *PARKS* **8(2)**.

Kenchington, R.A. (1988). Making a plan. In *Coral Reef Management Handbook*. UNESCO, Jakarta, Indonesia.

Kenchington, R.A. (1990). *Managing Marine Environments.* Taylor and Francis, New York.

Kenchington, R.A. and Agardy, T. (1990). Achieving Marine Conservation through Biosphere Reserve Planning and Management. *Environ. Cons.* **H(1)**: 39–44.

Lauck, T., Clark, C.W., Mangel, M. and Munro, G.R. (1998). Implementing the precautionary principle in fisheries management through marine reserves. *Ecol. Applic.*, **8(1)**, Suppl. S72–S78.

Norse, E. (ed) (1993). *Global Marine Biological Diversity: A Strategy for Building Conservation into Decision Making*. Center for Marine Conservation, IUCN, WWF, UNEP.

Nowlis, J.S. and Roberts, C.M. (1999). *Fisheries Benefits and Optimal Design of Nature Reserves*. Fishery Bulletin, in press.

Parks Canada (1986). *Marine National Parks Policy*. Environment Canada, Ottawa, Canada.

Russ, G.R. and Alcala, A.C. (1996). Do marine reserves export adult fish biomass? Evidence from Apo Island, Central Philippines. *Marine Ecology Progress Series* **132**: 1–9.

Salm, R.V. and Clark, J.R. (1984). *Marine and Coastal Protected Areas: A Guide for Planners and Managers*. IUCN, Gland, Switzerland.

Shackell, N.L. and Willison, J.H.M. (Eds) (1995). *Marine Protected Areas and Sustainable Fisheries*. Science and Management of Protected Areas Association, Wolfville, Nova Scotia, Canada.

Sherman, K. and Laughlin, T. (Eds) (1992). *The Large Marine Ecosystem (LME) Concept and its Application to Regional Marine Resource Management*. IUCN, Gland and Cambridge, UK.

Silva, M.E., Gately, E.M. and Desilvestre, I. (1986). *A bibliographic listing of coastal and marine protected areas: a global survey*. Woods Hole Oceanog. Inst. Tech. Rept. WHOI-86-11.

Task Force on Economic Benefits of Protected Areas of the World Commission on Protected Areas (WCPA) of IUCN, in collaboration with the Economics Service Unit of IUCN (1998). *Economic Values of Protected Areas: Guidelines for Protected Area Managers*. IUCN, Gland, Switzerland and Cambridge, UK.

UNESCO (1987). *A Practical Guide to MAB.* UNESCO, Paris.

Wells, S.N, McFieldy, M.D., Gibson, J., Carter, J. and Sedburry, G.R. (1995). *Marine protected areas in Belize and their potential in fisheries management.*

WWF-UK (1997). Particularly sensitive sea areas. *Marine Update.* WWF-UK, Godalming, UK.

WWF and IUCN (1998). *Creating a Sea Change – the WWF/IUCN Marine Policy.* WWF/IUCN.

Annex 6

Acronyms used

ACIUCN	Australian Committee for IUCN
ADB	Asian Development Bank
CBD	Convention on Biological Diversity
CCAMLR	Convention on the Conservation of Antarctic Marine Living Resources
CNPPA	(IUCN's) Commission on National Parks and Protected Areas (now WCPA)
EA	Environmental Assessment
EIA	Environmental Impact Assessment
EEZ	Exclusive Economic Zone
FAO	Food and Agricultural Organization of the United Nations
GBRMPA	Great Barrier Reef Marine Park Authority (Australia)
GEF	Global Environmental Facility
GESAMP	Joint Group of Experts on the Scientific Aspects of Marine Pollution
IMO	International Maritime Organization
ISBA	International Seabed Authority
IUCN	International Union for the Conservation of Nature and Natural Resources (now the World Conservation Union)
IWC	International Whaling Commission
LME	Large Marine Ecosystems
MAB	UNESCO's Man and the Biosphere Programme
MPA	Marine Protected Area
NOAA/NMFS	The National Oceanic and Atmospheric Administration/ National Marine Fisheries Service of the US Department of Commerce
PSSAs	Particularly Sensitive Sea Areas
SPREP	South Pacific Regional Environmental Programme
UNCLOS	United Nations Convention on the Law of the Sea
UNDP	United Nations Development Programme
UNEP	United Nations Environment Programme
UNESCO	United Nations Educational, Scientific and Cultural Organization
WCPA	World Commission on Protected Areas (of IUCN)
WWF	World Wide Fund for Nature (World Wildlife Fund in North America)